# Agent-Based Social Systems
# Volume 4

Series Editor: Hiroshi Deguchi, Yokohama, Japan

# ABSS — Agent-Based Social Systems

This series is intended to further the creation of the science of agent-based social systems, a field that is establishing itself as a transdisciplinary and cross-cultural science. The series will cover a broad spectrum of sciences, such as social systems theory, sociology, business administration, management information science, organization science, computational mathematical organization theory, economics, evolutionary economics, international political science, jurisprudence, policy science, socioinformation studies, cognitive science, artificial intelligence, complex adaptive systems theory, philosophy of science, and other related disciplines.

The series will provide a systematic study of the various new cross-cultural arenas of the human sciences. Such an approach has been successfully tried several times in the history of the modern sciences of humanities and systems and has helped to create such important conceptual frameworks and theories as cybernetics, synergetics, general systems theory, cognitive science, and complex adaptive systems.

We want to create a conceptual framework and design theory for socioeconomic systems of the twenty-first century in a cross-cultural and transdisciplinary context. For this purpose we plan to take an agent-based approach. Developed over the last decade, agent-based modeling is a new trend within the social sciences and is a child of the modern sciences of humanities and systems. In this series the term "agent-based" is used across a broad spectrum that includes not only the classical usage of the normative and rational agent but also an interpretive and subjective agent. We seek the antinomy of the macro and micro, subjective and rational, functional and structural, bottom-up and top-down, global and local, and structure and agency within the social sciences. Agent-based modeling includes both sides of these opposites. "Agent" is our grounding for modeling; simulation, theory, and real-world grounding are also required.

As an approach, agent-based simulation is an important tool for the new experimental fields of the social sciences; it can be used to provide explanations and decision support for real-world problems, and its theories include both conceptual and mathematical ones. A conceptual approach is vital for creating new frameworks of the worldview, and the mathematical approach is essential to clarify the logical structure of any new framework or model. Exploration of several different ways of real-world grounding is required for this approach. Other issues to be considered in the series include the systems design of this century's global and local socioeconomic systems.

Y. Shiozawa, Y. Nakajima, H. Matsui,
Y. Koyama, K. Taniguchi, F. Hashimoto

# Artificial Market Experiments with the U-Mart System

With 83 Figures, Including 5 in Color

Springer

Yoshinori Shiozawa
Kansai Urban Bank Professor
Graduate School of Management
Kyoto University
Yoshida-Honmachi, Sakyo-ku,
Kyoto 606-8501, Japan

Hiroyuki Matsui, Ph.D.
Associate Professor
Graduate School of Management
Kyoto University
Yoshida-Honmachi, Sakyo-ku,
Kyoto 606-8501, Japan

Kazuhisa Taniguchi, Ph.D.
Professor
Faculty of Economics
Kinki University
3-4-1 Kowakae, Higashiosaka,
Osaka 577-8502, Japan

Yoshihiro Nakajima, Ph.D.
Associate Professor
Graduate School of Economics
Osaka City University
3-3-138 Sugimoto, Sumiyoshi-ku,
Osaka 558-8585, Japan

Yusuke Koyama, Ph.D.
Assistant Professor
Department of Computational Intelligence
and Systems Science
Tokyo Institute of Technology
4259 Nagatsuta-cho, Midori-ku,
Yokohama 226-8503, Japan

Fumihiko Hashimoto
Professor
Graduate School of Economics
Osaka City University
3-3-138 Sugimoto, Sumiyoshi-ku,
Osaka 558-8585, Japan

ISSN 1861-0803
ISBN 978-4-431-54689-4 ISBN 978-4-431-76823-4 (eBook)

This is the English Translation from the Japanese Language Edition:
"Let's learn market Mechanism by Artificial Market"

Softcover re-print of the Hardcover 1st edition 2008


Springer is a part of Springer Science+Business Media
springer.com

Typesetting: Gravel Road Inc., Japan
Printing and binding: Hicom, Japan

Printed on acid-free paper

# Preface

U-Mart is a project that creates a virtual futures market on a stock index using a computer or network in order to promote on-site training, education, and even economics research. This book is aimed at students, teachers, and researchers, as well as individuals who are interested in stock and index futures trading, so that the U-Mart system can be widely utilized.

Please do not make a quick judgment and say, "This is mere stock trading experience software." Such software provided by some securities companies supposedly offers the user an opportunity to participate in the actual stock market, but the transactions made by users do not influence the stock price. In U-Mart, participants' behavior create the futures price. This is the essential difference between stock trading experience software and U-Mart.

The futures price varies depending on how the orders are placed, so the U-Mart can be regarded as a kind of game. Many students who have already participated in U-Mart as a part of the project have truly enjoyed U-Mart as a game.

Additionally, you can experience U-Mart by yourself. Read Chapter 1. It will enable you to use U-Mart starting completely from the beginner's level. In addition, if the operational environment is available, many people can participate through network in the U-Mart experiment as an actual game. How to use and play this game is described in Chapter 2. Chapter 3 describes a stock futures market so that individuals who have no knowledge of that market can understand what it is.

U-Mart has not been developed as a game, however. It is a research project to develop a new study tool for economics, on which economists and engineers can work together. See Chapter 6 regarding the significance of this research. As the research has progressed, we have gradually found that this system is superior as an educational tool.

On the economics side, users are able to learn what kinds of systems or structures move futures markets, and are strongly motivated to participate in the transactions. Refer to Chapter 3 for details. If you do not have any knowledge in this field, reading through this chapter will also give you a deeper understanding of futures markets. For teachers, U-Mart can be an experience-based educational program, providing strong motivation by taking 2 to 4 classroom hours in a two-unit lecture course.

U-Mart has been tried out in many universities as an educational program. If a teacher is willing to utilize U-Mart, a similar program can be conducted in high schools and junior high schools. The effect of this attempt is not merely to simulate stock trading and stock index trading. The futures market, internally, has a characteristic known as the zero-sum game. It is a world in which someone makes a profit while someone else takes a loss. Rather than teaching how to make money in the stock market, the U-Mart system offers the opportunity to reflect on what sort of structure the market has, and what kind of meaning profits and loss have to society as a whole. In this sense, the U-Mart system is also beneficial for education related to the financial market system.

In computer education, the U-Mart system provides a program of reasonable size and complexity, and in addition, the system has room for originality and ingenuity. Initially, the U-Mart system can be used to program a technical analysis-based agent as a machine agent. At more advanced levels, as a part of project-based education to build a market server of the U-Mart system, students are able to grasp the main points of system design in a network environment.

It is very important not only to experience the U-Mart system as a game, but also to analyze and examine the experimental results. As described in Chapter 1, you can start an experiment with U-Mart using just one computer. It is possible to obtain enormous quantities of experimental data conducting an accelerated experiment by using only machine agents. How can we analyze such vast amounts of data? This is the subject of the massive field of experimental design and statistics, and the initial suggestions are provided in Chapter 5.

The premise of this book is that anyone truly interested in U-Mart can experience it. Additionally, researchers and educators who are interested in computer-assisted education or multi-agent simulations can also benefit from the book when utilizing the U-Mart system. Chapter 2 describes detailed procedures for experiments conducted by several participants up to tens of participants in a network environment. Additionally, the source code is open. You can improve or modify the system by rewriting the source code under specific conditions. Chapter 4 is a report of an actual experiment played by human agents, i.e., ordinary people. This report can be used as a model on which a more advanced experimental plan can be designed.

As shown in other parts of this book, the U-Mart project was launched in 1999 with the aim of developing new study equipment for economics utilizing the latest achievements of the technologies of computer calculation and communication (ICT). For the history and results of U-Mart, please see our research group's Web site (http://www.u-mart.org/). The 7 years of activities have been organized into one pamphlet, published in Japanese and English. You can download this pamphlet from the Web site, and it is also on the accompanying CD-ROM.

The ultimate goal of U-Mart is to build research tools for financial market analysis and system design. The book does not refer to this goal directly; however, U-Mart has been utilized in many experiments conducted in Japanese universities, and a number of U-Mart experiments have also been conducted abroad. In the research field using the multi-agent model as a social experiment simulator, U-Mart has attained an international reputation as a dramatic development in this field, for the model has a firm grounding in the reality and has succeeded in the reconstruction of an actual economic situation. In fact, U-Mart is almost the only practical turnkey-based testbed for financial market research.

This book represents part of the achievements of a collaborative research group and plays a preparatory role to develop the U-Mart project on a wider range. With this book as a start, we hope that many people will become interested in U-Mart and multi-agent model simulations. The participation of new future researchers is heartily welcomed.

We could not have published this book without the contributions and cooperation of many people. It is impossible to cite all their names here, but the individuals named below were major leaders of the U-Mart project—our corroborative research associates and discussion fellows who devoted enormous efforts to the development of the U-Mart Server System and by consequence contributed in an essential way to the publication of this book: Isao Ono (Tokyo Institute of Technology), Hajime Kita (Kyoto University), Hiroshi Sato (National Defense Academy), Hiroshi Deguchi (Tokyo Institute of Technology), Takao Terano (Tokyo Institute of Technology), and Naoki Mori (Osaka Prefecture University). The U-Mart project could not have been created without the devoted participation of the above-named persons, who have contributed mainly on the engineering side of the project. Recently, the need for research that integrates the human sciences and natural sciences has been widely publicized, and we truly realize that this kind of collaborative research never yields results without interest and enthusiasm extending beyond the fields of both social science and engineering.

The U-Mart project was carried out with the help of a Grant-in-Aid for Scientific Research (Research No. 13224079, 14019076, 15017276, 16016274) and a research grant from the Foundation for the Fusion of Science and Technology.

The publication of this book was made possible with the assistance of a Grant-in-Aid for Scientific Research (Research No. 195208) and the 21st-Century COE Program "Creation of Agent-Based Social Systems Sciences (ABSSS)".

On behalf of the project group,<br>*Yoshinori Shiozawa*

July 2007

# Introduction — What is U-Mart?

UnReal Market as an Artificial Research Test bed (U-Mart) is an artificial futures market built by humans (human agents) and computer programs (machine agents), including trading tools. The following three activities are the main developments of U-Mart.

(1) Provides a common test bed for interdisciplinary research.
(2) Provides educational courseware for economics and engineering.
(3) Organizes open experiments domestically and internationally which connect research and education together.

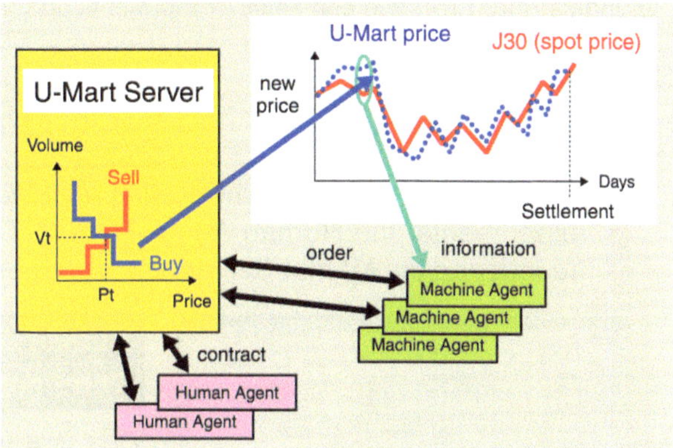


Recently, the research theme 'Artificial Market' has attracted a considerable amount of attention among engineers, mathematical scientists, as well as economists.

By using an artificial market, the U-Mart project was established with the aim of offering a forum or medium of exchange between economists and engineers. The project concept dates back to 1998. The U-Mart project was developed as a futures market simulator to trade on stock indexes. Many demonstrations have been conducted at various academic conferences and workshops including the Japan Association of Evolutionary Economics (JAEE). Additionally, remote experiments have been conducted, such as an experiment connecting the base universities in the Kanto and Kansai areas of Japan and also experiments with foreign countries. Many researchers participated in the U-Mart project, as one of the leading artificial market research projects in Japan. The U-Mart project covers a wide variety of aims and objectives, such as a system design for financial markets and market making operations, the degree of public information disclosure and range limitation, and the analysis of thin-board markets. The U-Mart simulator has a feature in which humans and computer programs can participate simultaneously in an experiment. Additionally, the simulator can make it possible to design a simulated market and actually run it. Hence, such economic experiments can be conducted to clarify trader's behavior regarding stock market transactions, market volatility, and market movement such as placement of wrong orders. Furthermore, in connection with this program creation, a wide variety of contributions to the field of engineering, such as evolutionary systems and adaptive learning, are expected.

# U-Mart System Overview

The U-Mart system offers an artificial futures market that humans (human agents) and computer programs (machine agents) can participate simultaneously in a market via a Local Area Network (LAN) or Internet. The U-Mart system provides several tools, from a transaction practice tool with a computer on hand to a tool that creates machine agents. Also the Human-Agent Trading Terminal and Market Server are tools prepared for experiments conducted in a network environment. The Market Simulator is a stand-alone software program, and the Log Analyzer is a tool that analyzes experimental results. The Human-Agent Trading Terminal, Market Server, and Market Simulator, are three tools that have almost the same graphical interface, and can share components and machine agents between each of the tools.

## Network Tools

Two tools are available when using a network structure to conducts experiments, the Human Agent Trading Terminal used by human traders and the Market Server acts as the exchange.

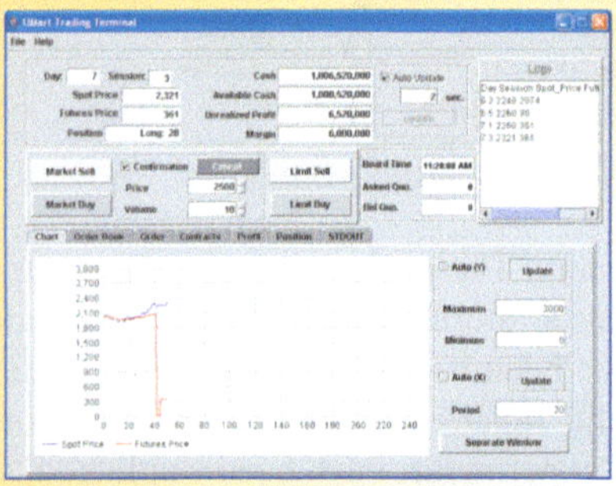

### Human-Agent Trading Terminal

This is a tool for human agents to participate in transactions. This tool displays various pieces of information the server offers, in addition to sending orders.

### Market Server

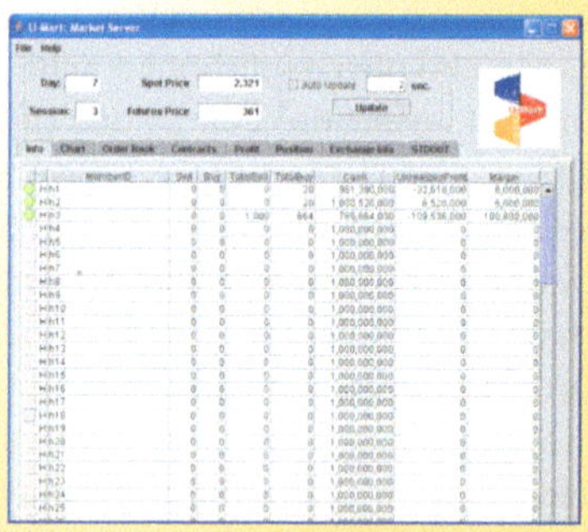

This is the core part of the U-Mart system. The Market Server acts as the market that establishes the transaction aggregated orders, and as the asset manager of the agents. The Market Server transmits a variety of data via the network, such data as market conditions, asset contents of each agent, and order movements. Additionally, the Market Server has the function of displaying this data. A machine agent can be embedded in advance.

## Stand-Alone Tool

This is a tool to practice futures trading with a computer on hand and to develop machine agents.

### Market Simulator

The market simulator is a practice tool to grasp the U-Mart trading overview and participate in transactions as a human agent. It has the same graphical interface as the human-agent trading terminal for the network. A human agent can have a machine agent that is embedded into U-Mart in advance as an opponent.

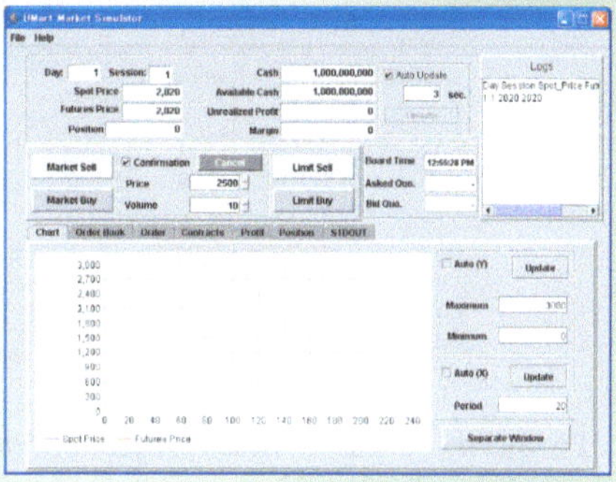


## Analysis Tool

This effective tool analyzes a vast amount of log data generated after an experiment. This tool can be used to analyze data from a wide range of viewpoints.

### Log Analyzer

The Log Analyzer is used when experimental results are to be analyzed. This tool can analyze the log output after an experiment to describe prices, turnovers, and positions graphically and it can track a participan's behavior. Additionally, the Log Analyzer is able to compare participant's behavior in order to analyze transaction results objectively.

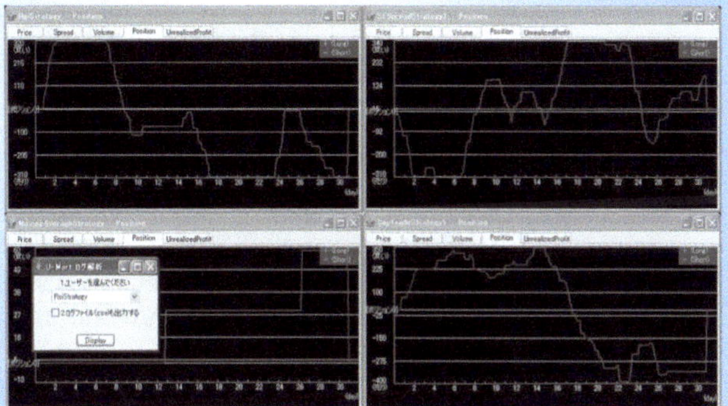

As mentioned above, the U-Mart tools were developed for research purposes and to be utilized in an academic educational setting. More than anything else, the actual operation of U-Mart leads to increased learning motivation through the participation in open market experiments. In the field of economics, U-Mart is utilized as a practical tool for experiencing financial market transactions and market analysis. In the field of engineering, U-Mart has been adopted as a programming drill. From very simple algorithm to a high-level learning algorithm or the implementation of a large scale program, U-Mart is able to set flexible goals according to each learning stage, and many good results have been obtained.

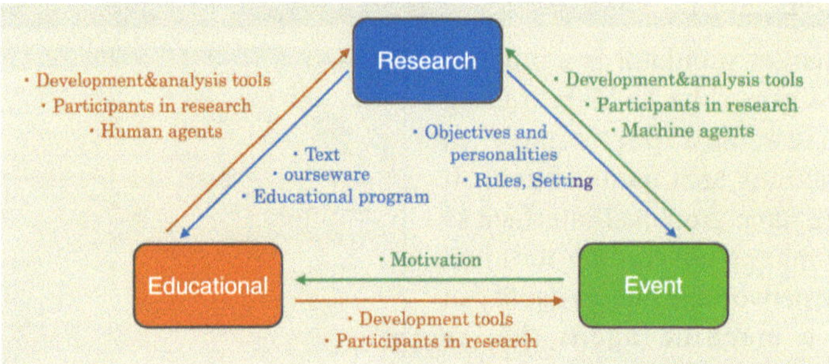


Furthermore, the U-Mart project conducts open experiments in order to connect research and education together. In the open experiments, vast amounts of experimental results and investment programs are collected, and the opportunities and data are offered to experimental participants for their research and education. Additionally, the U-Mart project provides researchers from different areas with a place to discuss and conduct corroborative studies. As just described, through interdisciplinary research and educational activities, the U-Mart project aims for establishment of a simulation study as a third research mode following theory and experiments.

We really hope that this book will be widely utilized, not only by university officials, but also by the general public.

June, 2007 *All the U-Mart project researchers*

**How to use this book**

1. Just start using U-Mart → Go to chapter one: "How to Use the U-Mart Market Simulator"
2. Conduct an experiment on a network → Go to chapter two: "How to Use the U-Mart System Network Edition"
3. Deepen your understand ding of the futures market → Go to chapter three: "Futures Market and U-Mart Experiments"
4. Conduct an experiment by humans for market analysis → Go to chapter four: "The Case of U-Mart Experiments by Human Agents" and chapter five: "Statistical Analysis of U-Mart Experiments by Humans"
5. Consider the meaning and future perspective of U-Mart → Go to chapter six: "Possibility and Meaning of U-Mart"

# Contents

# Part I
# Practice

# Chapter 1
# How to Use the U-Mart Market Simulator

## 1.1 The U-Mart System

The U-Mart system utilizes the following three types of tools in experiments by human agents: a market simulator, a market server and a trading terminal. Not much difference can be found among these three tools in their appearances and uses. In addition, a tool that uses only the machine agents to conduct experiments under various conditions (accelerating experiment support tool) are also prepared, as well as another tool for machine agents to participate in a transaction through a network (network adapter). This chapter gives an explanation as to how to use the market simulator. If you learn how to handle the market simulator, you will be able to make full use of the entire U-Mart system.[1]

The U-Mart market simulator is a tool for the practice of futures trading using an on-hand computer. Experiencing stock-index futures trading with preinstalled agents, the U-Mart system helps learners to deepen their understanding of the characteristics and regulations of markets in which many people participate such as stock markets, exchange markets and bond markets. The market server and trading terminal are tools that are utilized when several people participate in trading simultaneously within a network environment. Using these tools allows you to meet other trading opponents. The next chapter handles how to use these tools.[2]

---

[1] These tools have been developed when conducting an open experiment of the U-Mart or conducting various lectures using U-Mart. Most of these have been developed individually, so system designs, appearances, uses, and the system environments. Operating systems (OS) have yet to be integrated. At the publication of this book, Prof. Isao Ono of Tokyo Institute of Technology has redeveloped the U-Mart system. At the same time, Prof. Naoki Mori of Osaka City University has developed the graphic user interface (GUI) as part of the system in order to integrate the graphical interface.

[2] In the annual U-Mart open experiment, a trading competition, many university students and graduate students participated. In this experiment, professional investors also participated, with the machine agents those were developed in laboratory divisions which studied the production of support systems. Machine agents and human agents, on a fifty-fifty basis, have placed within the TOP 10 competitors during this annual competition over the past 4 years from 2002 to 2005. Just

You can find your own method of getting accustom to trading by using this system. By using the market simulator, you can try your investment strategy with a variety of conditions. You can configure conditions freely. For example, you can set conditions where a bubble or a stock plunge occurs, or where trends change. You can change a combination of machine agents as your opponent. In addition, you can create and install a machine agent that is programmed with your own investment strategy. Various kinds of data can be recorded for each transaction, such as price, trading volume, and orders. Trading contents can be analyzed with various analytical tools such as spreadsheet software.

## 1.2 Let Us Start

### *1.2.1 CD-ROM Setup*

The U-Mart system does not require an installation program. The market simulator and trading terminal can be started directly from the attached CD-ROM. You can freely conduct experiments even in a computer room of a university where such software installation maybe restricted. All the required programs can be started directly from the CD-ROM.

Or you may choose to copy of the contents of the CD-ROM to the hard disk. Running the program from the hard disk provides for faster access and increased program stability. Furthermore, making a copy allows saving log files (files that record price, orders, and transaction details) and configuration files. You can use the U-Mart system with any Java-friendly operating systems, such as Windows, Macintosh, Linux, and UNIX. Operation in Windows will be explained in the following section.

### *1.2.2 Run and Settings*

Let us start the U-Mart market simulator. Double-click on the file 'MarketSimulator_en.exe.' For U-Mart tools, the English version is prepared in addition to the Japanese version. Execute 'MarketSimulator_en.exe' when you want to use the English version because the boot file is different depending on each language. The notations in the programs are different between English and Japanese versions, while how to use and available information are similar. The English version will be used from the following section. For the other tools, both English and Japanese versions are prepared.

like the computer chess program called Deep Blue that defeated the human chess master, can we expect whether there appears the strongest machine agent in the future?

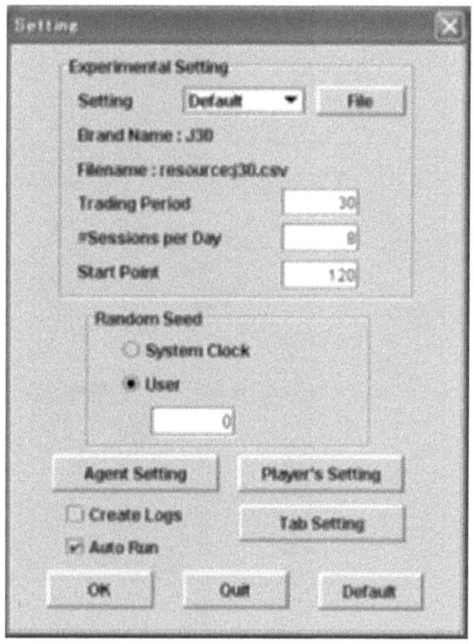


**Fig. 1.1** Setting Dialogue Box

The settings dialogue box is displayed when starting the U-Mart market simulator (Fig. 1.1). Here, you can configure price data that is used as a spot price, trading period, trading times per day (called sessions) and so forth. When clicking on the 'Agent Setting' button, the combination of machine agents participating together in the futures market (U-Mart) and the parameter settings file that configures machine agents' behavior can be loaded. Using different settings and how to make configuration files are handled in the next chapter. At this point clicking on the "OK" button without changing anything will start the U-Mart Market Simulator.

### *1.2.3 Date and Session*

A window like in Fig. 1.2 will be displayed when the U-Mart market is started. The upper half of the window displays constant information and order buttons, and the lower half displays individual's asset conditions, market information, and various pieces of information needed for trading. Such information can be changed by selecting the respective tabs.

See the two boxes in the upper left in Fig. 1.3. The textbox 'Day' displays the present day and the 'Session' textbox displays the present session number. The market is configured to progress automatically every three seconds by default. In the upper right, the textboxes and buttons are placed to configure the market progress speed (Fig. 1.4). The market stops progressing by unchecking the 'Auto Update' checkbox. It will resume progressing automatically when checking the checkbox again.[3] The progress speed can be adjusted by changing the index in the textbox

[3] When conducting a network experiment described in the next chapter, the market progress is managed by the market server. A trading tool called "trading terminal" for network experiments

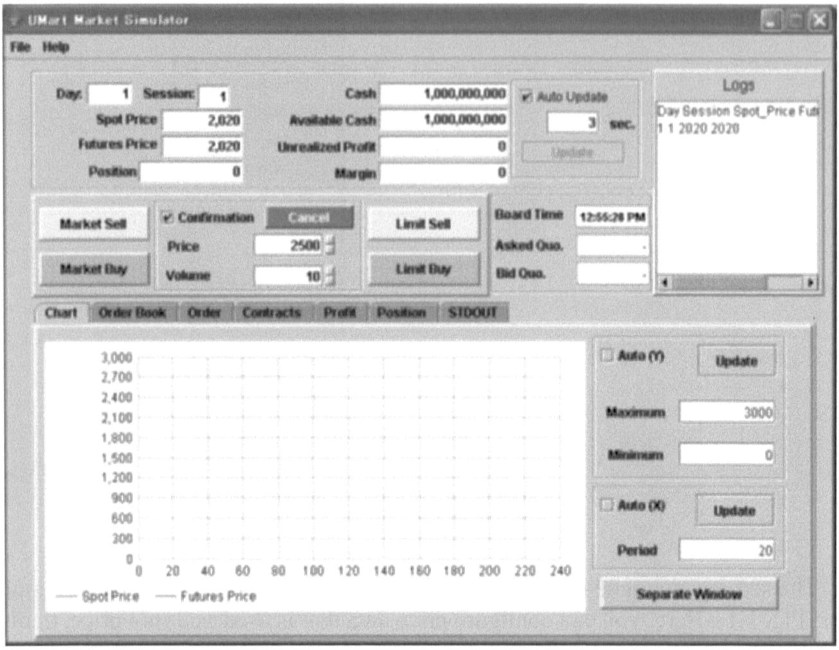


**Fig. 1.2** Market Simulator GUI

**Fig. 1.3** Index information panel

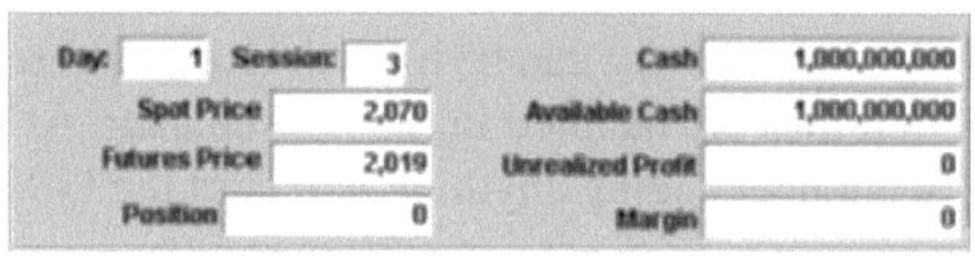


**Fig. 1.4** Time management panel

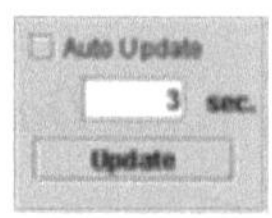


below. Uncheck the 'Auto Update' checkbox once, and set the updating interval as 0.1 seconds. Check the automatic updating checkbox again, and then the market starts progressing at higher speed. Again, uncheck the 'Auto Update' checkbox. Every time the 'Update' button is clicked, the market progresses by one session.[4] Now reset the system settings to update automatically every three seconds.

has a similar window configuration as the market simulator explained in this chapter, the buttons and windows are set in this way. In the trading terminal, these buttons and windows are used to control the update timing of price and order books. Caution, the buttons are the same, but their functions are different.

[4] When clicking the 'Update' button at the last session of a day (the eighth session in this case), the program mode is changed into the after-trading hours. A detailed explanation about the after-trading hours will be given later.

**Fig. 1.5** Logs window

During every session, trading is established with settlement of prices according to the orders placed by agents participating in this futures market. The latest spot price is displayed in the 'Spot Price' textbox, and the future price decided in the previous session is displayed in the 'Futures Price' textbox, respectively. In the market simulator, previous data from Japan's stock index J30 provided by Mainichi Shimbun was embedded as the price time series of actual market. Moreover, 10 different types of investment programs (machine agents) are also preinstalled as trading opponents.

Counting the orders placed by machine agents and players at the end of a session, the *Itayose* method is used to set prices and conduct trading. When an order placed by an agent is established, it means that "the order has been contracted."[5] The futures price decided here is displayed in the textbox 'Futures Price.' Where trading is not conducted, '-' is displayed in the textbox. The 'Logs' window on the right side displays the previous price series (Fig. 1.5). On each line, the following information is displayed from the left to right: date, session, spot price, and futures price.

As a player participating in the market, your asset conditions are the rest of basic information. The 'Position' textbox displays the number of positions you are having. Additionally, each textbox such as 'Cash,' 'Available Cash,' 'Unrealized Profit,' and 'Margin' displays the breakdown of your account. Detailed description regarding this will be given later.

### *1.2.4 Placing Orders*

Let us place an order. There are some buttons and windows for ordering in the center of the window (Fig. 1.6). Buying and selling futures orders can be placed by clicking on the 'Market Sell' or 'Market Buy.' Click on the sell button several time for the proper timing after confirming that the market is updating automatically. When futures trading is established, the 'Position' textbox displays "short:10" , "long:7" In addition, once you have a position, the indexes in the textboxes of 'Cash,' 'Available Cash,' 'Unrealized Profit,' and 'Margin' will change at the end of each day.

[5] The detailed explanation regarding the *Itayose* will be given in chapter 3. Section 4 in this chapter also explains the basics related to the *Itayose* method when describing an order book.

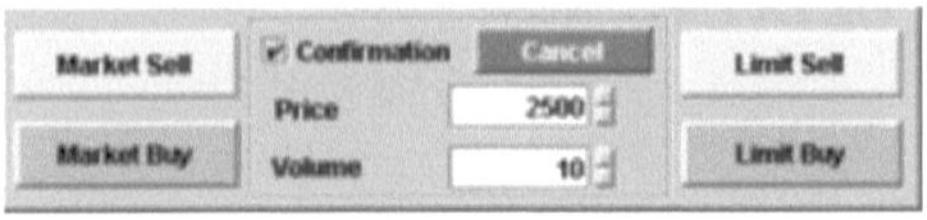


**Fig. 1.6** Order panel

### *1.2.5 Various Tabs*

The display of the bottom half of the window is changed according to which tab is selected. Watch how the market moves by selecting various tabs such as Chart, Order Book, or Contracts. The 'Chart' tab is opened by default and displays the price chart. The blue line of the chart indicates the spot price, and the red one indicates the futures price. When selecting the 'Order Book' tab, an order book that lists the orders placed by you and other machine agents is displayed. There are some other windows to confirm the changes in your asset conditions, for example, order, contract, and position information. The chart can be displayed in a separated window by clicking on the 'Separate Window' button, which is displayed in the Chart, Profit, and Position tabs. Furthermore, by checking the checkboxes 'Auto (Y)' and 'Auto (X),' the chart can be enlarged to show more detailed movements. The trading period of this experimental setting is set for 30 days. Try placing an order before a trading period ends, and confirm what happened by using tabs and buttons.

### *1.2.6 Final Settlement*

A settlement will take place after 30 days of trading has ended. All the positions are settled by the first spot price of the day 31*st* (called Special Quotation), then the final profit is determined.[6] Confirm whether the 'Final Result' window appears. Your results are listed at the top. A profit can be realized only when the result is over one billion yen. Anything less than one billion yen is considered a loss.

### *1.2.7 Quitting*

Let us quit the market. Click on the 'OK' button of the 'Final Result' window. Then, select 'Quit' from the file menu in the upper left corner of the Market Simulator window. You can quit the program by clicking 'OK' in the confirmation pop-up window that is displayed. Did you understand the basic workings of U-Mart? The next section gives you some tips for understanding how to conduct specific trading, the mechanism of a futures market, and how to use the U-Mart tools and information.

[6] All the positions are cleared, and netting is conducted. Moreover, all margin money is also returned. See chapter 3 for a more detailed explanation.

## 1.3 Let Us Trade

This section is hands-on and real-time operation of the system. Please follow the instructions carefully. In this section you will be given a detailed explanation regarding the mechanism of futures markets and how to use the market simulator, and its information.

### *1.3.1 Settings*

Start the market simulator once again. Let us change some settings in the settings dialogue box (Fig. 1.7). Select Ex2 from the setting pull-down menu of 'Experimental Setting.' Confirm that the 'Trading Period' textbox is set to 10 days; 'Session per Day' is set to 8 times; 'Starting Point' is set at 400, respectively.[7] Then next, confirm that the 'User' radio button is checked in 'Random Seed' panel and the index '0' is entered in the textbox.[8] Auto run checkbox should be unchecked. Leaving the other settings unchanged, and then click on 'OK.'[9]

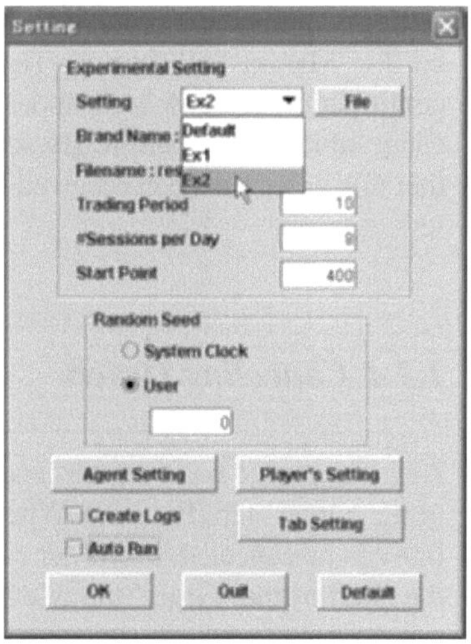


**Fig. 1.7** Setting dialogue box

---

[7] The configuration files that defile time series and experimental setting can be loaded by clicking on File next to the setting pull-down menu. A variety of market simulations will be available by replacing the time series files. See chapter 2 regarding how to create the settings files.

[8] By specifying the Random Seed, machine agent behavior can be replicated. Additionally, when specifying a different Random Seed, the order of ordering and agent orders will be changed even when using the same agent combination.

[9] You can select a member list that you compete against, by clicking the 'Agent Setting' button. In addition, player's competition conditions, such as player's initial assets, can be changed by clicking the 'Player's Setting' button. From the 'Tab Setting' button, different tab windows can be selected.

### 1.3.2 Futures Trading

In futures trading, futures product volume is counted as a 'unit,' such as "one unit, two units" (*Mai*, in Japanese). Buying one unit of a futures product in U-Mart means to contract to buy out underlying asset (stock package of J30 in the U-Mart) with the price of 1,000 times points until the due date. For example, where one unit is contracted at 2,625 points, it means that the trade equals to an amount of 2,625,000 yen (2,625 $\times$ 1,000 = 2,625,000). We seldom conduct such transactions with such a large amount of money; however, you can feel at ease to place orders of this size since you have one billion yen in your account initially.

### 1.3.3 Placing Orders

Make sure that the 'Auto run' checkbox is unchecked, and then click on the 'Update' button. Progress in time until "Day 3" and "Session 3" is displayed. By looking at the chart, it indicates that the market is now in a downward trend. To observe the chart more precisely, check the 'Auto (Y)' checkbox. The chart can be enlarged by clicking on the 'Update' button. At this point, let us place a sell order. The order setting window and order buttons are located in the center of the window. Click on the 'Market Sell' button. The order amount is set to 10 units by default, so a confirmation window will appear to confirm placing a 10-unit market sell order. Click on the 'OK' button. By selecting the order tab, you can select the order tab that this order has been received by the exchange and the Order ID number is set at 251.[10]

### 1.3.4 Canceling Orders

An order placed once can be canceled. The 'Cancel' line is located on the very right of the 'Order' tab (Fig. 1.8). When checking the checkbox here, all the orders in this line can be canceled.[11] If order canceling is successful, the order line specified from the chart of the 'Order' tab will be erased. Select the 'Contracts' tab. Index '10' is

[10] In the market simulator, just as doing now, you can place an order stopping a time freely and confirming what is going on. When conducting trading with the automatic updating function, however, it is important when the order should be placed. Orders can be placed with shortcut keys. Alt+S is assigned to Market Sell, Ctrl+S to Limit Sell, Alt+B to Market Buy, and Ctrl+B to Limit Buy. Additionally, orders can be placed without confirmation window by unchecking the 'Confirmation' checkbox next to the 'Cancel' button.

[11] You can cancel your order by using the 'Cancel' button in the 'Price' window, which is to the right center of the order buttons. The Order ID identification dialogue box appears when this cancel button is clicked. Enter your Order ID here.

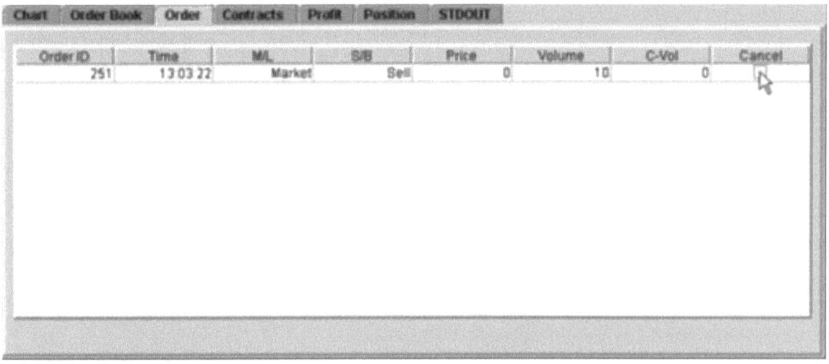


**Fig. 1.8** 'Order' tab. An order can be canceled by checking the 'Cancel' checkbox

input in the 'Can-Vol' column of Order ID 251. This now confirms that the order has been canceled.

## 1.4 Orders and Contract

### *1.4.1 Market and Limit Order*

Let us place a market sell order of 10 units once again. Order ID this time is 252. There are two ways to place an order: market order and limit order. A market order means to place an order for buying or selling the amount of units needed regardless of the price. Many books for beginner stock investors often mention that beginners should place a market order in principle. The market order is easily received when a player wants to buy or sell; however, sometimes the player buys at a high price or sells at a low price in an unexpected way. On the other hand, a limit order is an order that specifies the highest (or lowest) buy (or sell) price below (or above) the original investment price. The limit order is a comparatively safe way, because it is able to restrict selling and buying prices. However, this order method has the possibility of missing out on the optimum time to buy or sell.[12]

Now click the 'Update' button once. This causes the third *Itayose* session to be concluded and to advance the order time to the fourth session. Where the order that was placed earlier is contracted, the order contents are reflected in the 'Contracts' tab (Fig. 1.9). The order that was placed earlier, all 10 units, have been contracted with 1,864 points.

[12] U-Mart version 2.0 that is introduced now no longer has a circuit breaker system which limits price movement and updates indicative prices. Additionally, since trading is conducted with the *Itayose* method, extremely low or high prices are obtained in some cases. It might be better to place a limit order first.

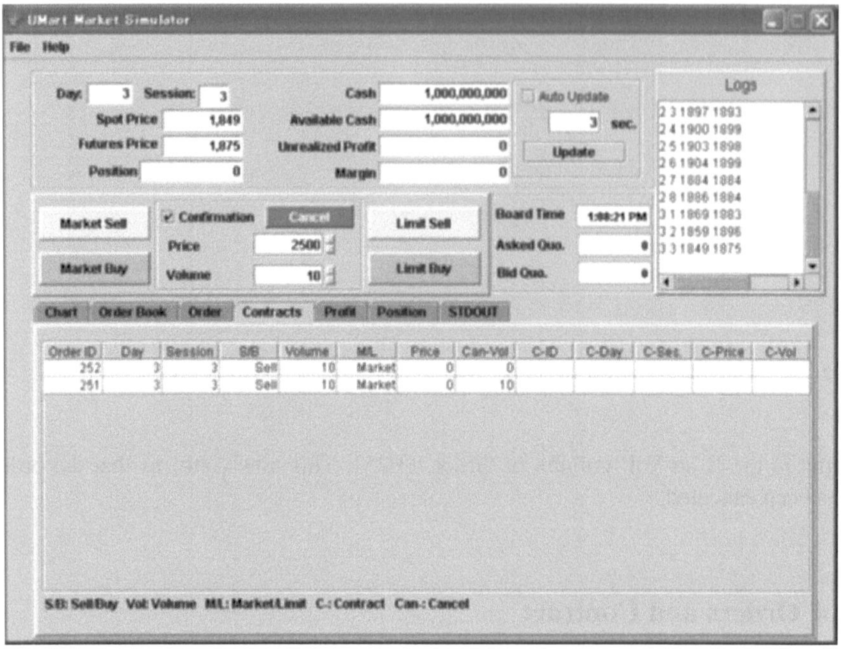


**Fig. 1.9** “Contacts” tab

*Open Interests (Contracts)*

Now the agreement to sell 10 units of J30 on the settlement day ($11^{th}$ morning, in this case) has been made, namely, it has promised to sell the stocks for 18,640,000 yen (1,864 points $\times$ 1,000 volumes $\times$ 10 units). In futures market, this is called ‘Open Interest’ (Contract). Buying futures products is called ‘Purchase Contract,’ and selling is called ‘Sales Contract.’ A substantial balance of purchase and sales contracts is referred to as a ‘partial position.’ Setting a selling account is called ‘short,’ and a partial sales position that is held is called “short position.” Now you have 10 short positions since the selling order placed earlier has been contracted. Confirm that the ‘Position’ window displays as “short:10.” Similarly, a partial purchase position that is held is called “long position.” When holding 12 long positions, it is displayed as “long: 12.”

## *1.4.2 Guarantee System*

In futures trading, only the agreement for the trade on a clearing day is exchanged. In principle, no cash transaction takes place on site. Because of this, it cannot be known whether the agreement is absolutely implemented or not, since anybody can enter the market. For this reason, generally, there are two systems adopted in the futures

**Table 1.1** Futures Trading Guarantee System

| Guarantee System | Price | Timing | Method |
|---|---|---|---|
| Margin | 300,000 yen per 1 unit | When contracted | Available cash changes |
| Mark-to-Market | Difference between contracted price and the closing price of the day | After a day finished | Cash changes |

market to insure that orders are settled. One is "Margin System," and the other is "Mark-to-Market." Margin money is calculated when futures trading is contracted. On the other hand, Mark-to-Market is conducted when trading for a day is finished. See the following Table 1.1.

*Margin System*

First, let us consider margin money or trading margin requirements. These are assets deposited in the exchange in order that futures settlements can be implemented properly. By default of the U-Mart, margin money is configured as 300,000 yen per one partial position.[13]

Margin money is transferred to the exchange every time the partial position increases or decreases. In the case of U-Mart, any cash transaction related to margin money is not performed since all money is preliminarily deposited in the account. However, the money amount that should be secured as margin money from the cash account is automatically calculated as well as the money amount you can move freely considering margin money, and both money amounts are clearly divided. From cash, the money amount that can not be used as margin money is displayed in the 'Margin' textbox, and the money amount being removed as margin money from cash is displayed in the 'Available Cash' textbox.

When the partial position increases, for one unit, margin money has a 300,000 yen increase and available cash has a 300,000 yen decrease. Since 10 units were contracted this time, cash remains at the default price of one billion yen. However, the margin is 3,000,000 yen and available cash is 997,000,000 yen. Now confirm these changes by looking at each respective window.

[13] The margin system depends on exchanges and stock brands. It is popular to put down a fixed margin per one partial position. For example, one unit of gold futures listed on The Tokyo Commodity Exchange requires margin money of 60,000 yen. Recently, the exchanges adopting Standard Portfolio Analysis of Risk (SPAN(R)) that was developed by Chicago Mercantile Exchange (CME) have been increased. For multiple products listed on the same exchange, this system deducts the portion that can be counterbalanced with the up-and-down of market price, and calculates margin money according to the risk the entire portfolio has. Both exchanges, Osaka Securities Exchange on which Nikkei 225 future is listed and Tokyo Stock Exchange on which TOPIX future is listed, adopted SPAN(R) on the 30$^{th}$ of October, 2000.

*Mark-to-Market*

Another guarantee system is Mark-to-Market. In futures trading, someone's sale corresponds to someone's purchase, so the total number of sales and purchase contracts are equivalent. For that reason, someone's profit corresponds to someone's loss. The profit and loss are aggregated on the settlement day when the futures were traded. In order to guarantee this, the Mark-to-Market system clears profits and losses with cash every day.

Click on the 'Update' button. After clicking four times, you will be able to move on to the order time of the eighth session on the third day. By clicking the 'Update' button once again, brings about the end of the eighth session. You can confirm this by seeing the session number turn to '-'. This mark indicates that it is now after-trading hours. On the last button click, the Mark-to-Market transaction was conducted based on the futures price (closing price) of the final session of the day, in addition to the usual *Itayose* operation of the eighth session, that updates the positions and margin of each agent was performed. The price determined at the final session has a special meaning. Unrealized profit and loss is calculated comparing the position price currently being held and the closing price of the day. Then the calculated price is transferred in cash. Cash is received where profit is realized, whereas cash is paid out where a loss is realized.[14] Margin money keeps cash in the account, whereas cash transfers to and from the accounts of the agents conducting futures trading.

In the fifth session on the third day, 10 units were shorted at 1,864 points. The price was dropped 19 points from the trading price of 1,864 since the price determined at the eighth session was 1,845. Here, the unrealized profit and loss is worth about 190,000 yen ((1,864 points $-$ 1,845 points) $\times$ 1,000 $\times$ 10 units). In futures trading, the number of short and long positions in the entire market is always equal. Hence, observing the entire market, you can see 10 units of a long position at the same price, and an unrealized loss (appraisal loss) is suffered at the same price as what was have gained. Next the cash transfer occurs. It is collected from the account taking the unrealized loss, and transferred to the account of an agent who gained the unrealized profit. Now confirm the price 190,000 yen is displayed in the 'Unrealized Profit' textbox, and cash is increased to 100,190,000 yen with 190,000 yen increased in cash.

### 1.4.3 Bankruptcy

When it becomes impossible for an agent to prepare cash for Mark-to-Market, the agent goes bankrupt. Notice that it is not when taking a loss of over one billion yen.

[14] Mark-to-Market is also conducted upon the profit and loss ending the previous day. On this point, the money transactions of the day are performed with the difference between the closing prices of previous day and current day regarding the position being held earlier. When it comes to the position contracted on the current day, the money transaction is performed with the difference between contracted and closing prices.

Systematically, you can hold a partial position in the range of 'available cash divided 300,000 yen,' and you have one billion yen in cash when U-Mart trading is begun without changing the default settings. This means that you can make positions until 3,333 units (1,000,000,000 yen / 300,000 yen) because margin money is 300,000 yen per one unit. Let us suppose you have 2,000 long positions. At this time, the exchange holds six billion yen (2,000 × 300,000 yen). If the closing price of the day drops one point below the exchange rate (purchase price), 2,000,000 yen of cash (1 point × 2,000 units × 1,000) will be withdrawn when Mark-to-Market is conducted. Since four billion yen is allotted as available cash, the cash for Mark-to-Market cannot be prepared if the price drops over 200 points (400,000,000 yen / 2,000,000 yen). In the futures market or stock market, it is quite normal to see certain large percentage price level movements like this within one day. Therefore, you need to observe your available cash and positions well so that you can understand to what extent of price movements you can withstand.[15]

## 1.5 Closed Trade

While observing the chart, let us again progress the market by clicking on the 'Update' button. Both spot and futures prices continue falling, repeatedly moving up-and-down. The unrealized profit and loss also vary from day to day in accordance with the futures price fluctuations. Entering the fourth day, the futures price drops to 1,800 points. Now let us conduct closed trade at this point in order to determine a part of the profits.

In futures trading, settlement is conducted with monetary compensation on the settlement day, which is referred to as 'Netting.' However, the settlement can be conducted in advance executing an opposite trade on the position (closed trade). You have 10 units of short positions now, so let us buy back the half of them, five units. This time, a limit buy order is placed. Progress the market until the third session of the fourth day by clicking on the 'Update' button. Let us place the five-unit buy order with 1,800 points because the futures price set upon the second session on this day was 1,771 points. Enter the index '1,800' in the 'Price' textbox and '5' in the 'Volume' textbox. To change the index in the 'Price' and 'Volume' textboxes, you can enter the index by selecting the window directly, or you can change the index by clicking on the index-change buttons located next to the 'Volume' textbox. The order is placed after confirming the order contents with the confirmation dialogue box that appears when clicking the 'Limit Buy' button (Fig. 1.10). Now you can confirm that the Order ID which is 353 now in the 'Order' window. The closed trade serves to determine the profit and loss, and to control a position in order to avoid going bankrupt due to unexpected price movements. Click on the 'Update' button once.

---

[15] According to the price movements in J30 for 2,444 days, during 29 Dec 1989 to 29 Nov 1999, the average fluctuation band of a day was 23.8 points, and the standard deviation was 25.4 points.

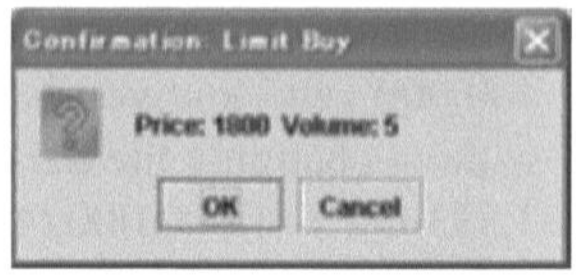


**Fig. 1.10** Confirmation dialogue box of a limit buy order

Now, the index in the ‘Position’ window has turned into ‘Short: 5,’ and the ‘Margin’ index has declined to 1,500,000 yen. Additionally, ‘Unrealized Profit’ remains in 190,000 yen because Mark-to-Market on the fourth day has not been conducted yet. Now finish the fourth-day of trading by clicking on the ‘Update’ button five times. Now the ‘Unrealized Profit’ has turned into 735,000 yen.

## *1.5.1 Order Book*

A limit order is an order that specifies the lowest selling price or the highest buying price. For that reason, the limit price and contract price of actual trading are different. Depending on the market situations, there may be a possibility of buying and selling of unexpected profitable prices. Progress the market to the third session of the sixth day by clicking on the ‘Update’ button, then select the ‘Book Order’ tab (Fig. 1.11). The chart on the left lists the orders of this session. Select ‘Simple’ from the choices of buttons. The orders placed by each agent are listed in the ‘Current Order Book.’ Let us try placing 10 units of a buy order with 1,770 points. The new line of 1,770 points will be added in the chart of the order book, and it will show that 10 units of a buy order have been placed.

When selecting ‘Sum,’ the total number of both buy and sell orders are displayed (Fig. 1.12). Since the limit buy order is intended to purchase when the price is below the limit price, a buy order is added from the one having a high price to the one having a low price in order. In contrast, a sell order is added from a low price, because the orders are transacted at a higher price than the limit price. According to this chart, the supply and demand curves are plotted. The figure on the right of the book order window shows the demand curve (red) and the supply curve (blue) from

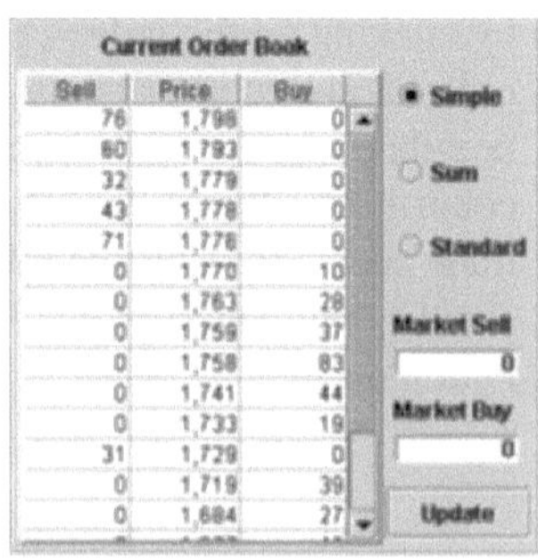


**Fig. 1.11** Order book of the third session on the sixth day (Simple)

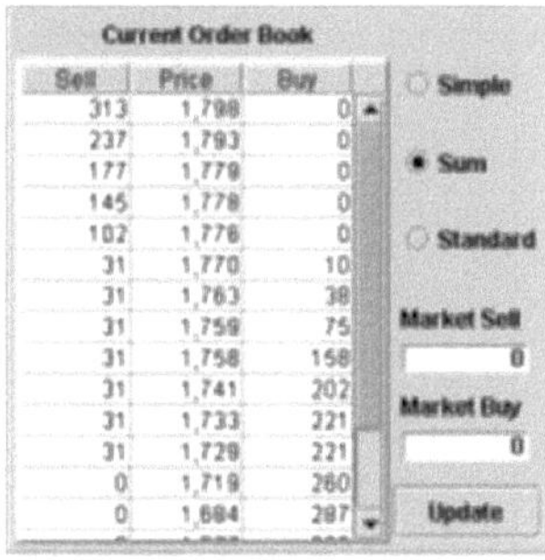


**Fig. 1.12** Order book of the third session on the sixth day (Sum)

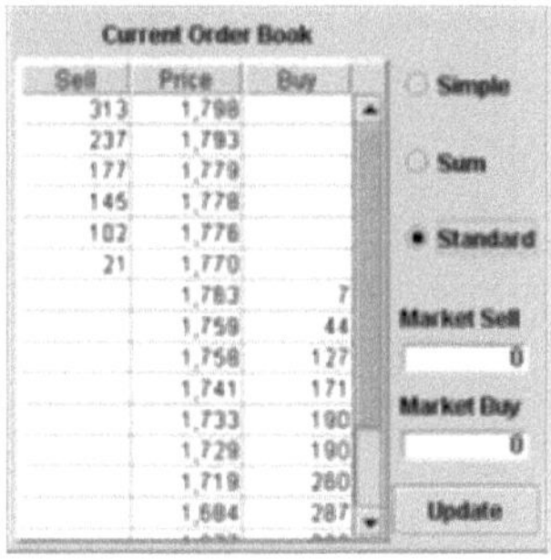


**Fig. 1.13** Order book of the third session on the sixth day (Standard)

the *Itayose* trading session conducted during the previous session. The contract price and the number of contracts are determined at the point where both curves cross.

The number of orders remaining after deducting sell orders from buy orders is displayed when 'Standard' is selected, from the 'Sum' chart (Fig. 1.13). Utilizing the order book provides such information as "the price that is about to be determined in this session," "the volume that can bought or sold without changing prices significantly" and "the order volume required to change the price significantly." Place 50 units of buy order with the same points, 1,770 to confirm that the order book changes. The standard window shows that there are 29 units of buy order with 1,770 points remaining. Selecting the 'Order' tab displays the Order ID placed in this session as 549 and 550.

## *1.5.2 Partial Contracts*

When orders are placed, not all orders are always contracted. Out of 60 units of buy order with 1,770 points in this case, 31 units were contracted but 29 units remained. Click on the 'Update' button. Selecting the 'Order' tab, you can see that ID 549 has 0 contracts and ID 550 has 31 contracts. Let us confirm the contract prices and contract volume by selecting the 'Contracts' tab (Fig. 1.14). As just described, it is refers to 'Partial Contracts' and show that only part of the placed orders were contracted.

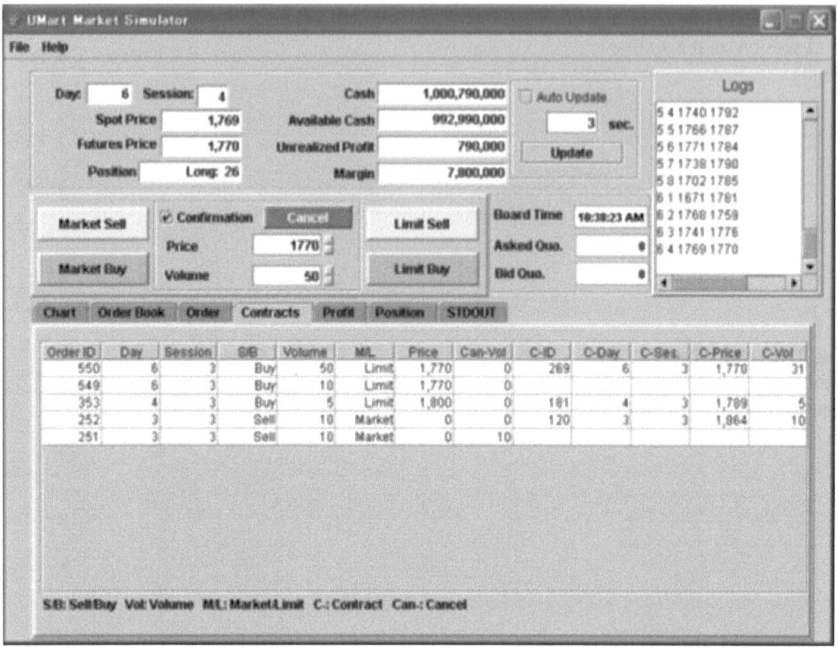

**Fig. 1.14** Contracts information

In U-Mart, an order placed once is valid for one day. When an order is contracted partially, the order remains until the next session unless the rest of orders are canceled. In this case, 29 units of buy order with 1,770 points were placed in the *Itayose* trading session by the fourth session. Conduct the fourth *Itayose* trading session by clicking on the 'Update' button once again. The price has gone down to 1,767 points. Now ID 550 has 19 units of a buy order and ID 549 has 2 units of a buy order, with a total, 21 units have been contracted.

The reason the order ID and contract ID ('C-ID' column) are given separately is that orders placed once can be contracted twice.[16] The machine agents that are embedded in the U-Mart system place orders without much consideration of the passage of time on the board, so the order volume of the first *Itayose* trading session is least. Hence, there is the tendency that the board becomes thick as it progresses. It is better to place the orders during the final part of a day if you want to trade a large volume with the same price.[17] On the contrary, the prices easily fluctuate when many orders are placed during the first *Itayose* trading session.

[16] There can be the case where an order is placed twice contracted at once. In such a case, separated contract IDs are given.

[17] In the actual futures market and stock market, the significant trading volume is observed in the "opening session" when the first price that is placed and the "closing session" which takes place at the final part of the day. This is referred to as V effect or W effect (since trading volume increases before and after the noon recess).

## 1.6 Various Information

All the sections up to this point have described the minimum required operations and how to view information. From this section forward, the explanation of individual operational panels is given.

### *1.6.1 Other Textboxes*

The three textboxes are displayed below the 'Update' button. The 'Board Time' textbox displays the current time (Fig. 1.15). The 'Asked Quo.' and 'Bid Quo.' display 0 usually, but they display quote prices when no trading is conducted at all. A quote price is a money amount that can be bought or sold at a certain price. When trading is conducted with the *Itayose* method, the quote price means the highest buying price and the lowest selling price when selecting 'Standard' from the order book. These textboxes display 0 when futures' trading is conducted, namely, when the futures prices are already decided. This information may help when the 'Order Book' tab is invalid.

### *1.6.2 Chart*

The chart that shows spot and futures prices is displayed. The vertical axis (Y axis) indicates price and the horizontal axis (X axis) indicates time. The Y axis is configured between 0 and 3,000 points at the default. Imputing the point indexes in the 'Maximum' and 'Minimum' textboxes, the range of the chart can be changed after clicking the 'Update' button. In addition, when the 'Update' button is clicked on by checking the 'Auto (Y)' checkbox, it automatically displays the adjusted chart between the lowest and the highest prices of the period. Just give it a try once.

The X axis is determined according to the experimental conditions when the experiment begins. All the sessions, from start to end, are displayed. When the 'Update' button is clicked on checking the 'Auto (X)' checkbox, the most recent 20 sessions are displayed. As time progresses, the chart also moves automatically. The chart range that is displayed can be adjusted by imputing a period index in the 'Period' textbox. Those people making good use of the automatic adjustment function have tended to have the result of earning a good trading mark. You may find the best way to display the chart by trying various ways.

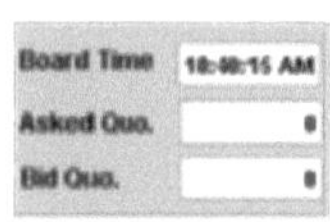


**Fig. 1.15** Board time and indicative prices panel

The chart is displayed in a separate window by clicking on the Separate window button. (Fig. 1.16)

### 1.6.3 Order Book

The order book shows board information on the left, and shows the board chart of the previous *Itayose* trading session on the right. There are three different methods to show board information. The 'Simple' view lists order information. The 'Sum' view lists the buying order volume accumulated from a higher price to a lower price, and the selling order volume accumulated from a lower price to a higher price. In the 'Standard' view, the total number of cumulative buy and sell orders are displayed. The 'Market Sell' and 'Market Buy' textboxes display the number of market orders that are currently placed, for each. The latest board information is available by clicking on the 'Update' button.

By default, the chart on the left aligns each chart item in order of 'Sell,' 'Price' and 'Buy,' respectively. You can rearrange each item freely by dragging the item tabs to the desire arrangement (Fig. 1.17). Additionally, an item can be sorted by double clicking on its item tab. Not only the order book, but also all the charts such as in the market simulator and the trading terminal have the same kind of function.

The line chart indicates information when the previous *Itayose* trading session was conducted. The blue line indicates the sell orders and the red line indicates the buy orders, in the 'Sum' view of the order book. The Y axis is volume and the X

**Fig. 1.16** Chart displayed in a separate window

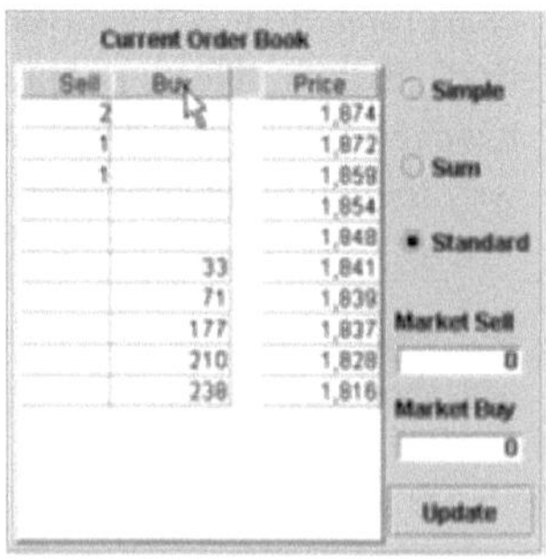


**Fig. 1.17** Change in the chart items

axis is the price by default. This X axis and Y axis can be rearranged when the 'Exchange X-Y' button is clicked. The following information is displayed: the date and session number of the line chart, the contracted price and volume at that time.

### *1.6.4 Contracts Information*

The 'Order' tab displays the orders that were placed within the current day. Display contents are cleared each time a day ends. This tab is selected when confirming the currently remaining orders and canceling orders. All the past order results are displayed by selecting the 'Contracts' tab. The number of cancelled orders, and contracts results are also displayed. As in the case of other charts, each chart item can be rearranged by dragging it to the desired arrangement. In addition, double clicking on each item tab allows the items to be sorted.

### *1.6.5 Profits*

The time series graph of 'Unrealized Profit' is displayed by selecting the 'Profit' tab. If positions are unchanged, the graph moves according to the futures price. Differing from the 'Chart' and 'Position' charts, the unrealized profit is calculated and updated not every *Itayose* sessions, but at daily intervals. The vertical axis (Y axis) indicates the unrealized profit, and the horizontal axis (X axis) indicates the time. The Y axis range is set from + 1,000,000,000 yen to – 1,000,000,000 yen. This range can be freely specified by imputing indexes in the 'Maximum' and 'Minimum' textboxes. When checking the 'Auto (Y)' and 'Auto (X)' checkboxes, data is plotted on the graph between maximum and minimum profit values of the specified period. In some cases, the Y axis is indicated in the price form. 2.24E7 expresses '$2.27 \times 10^7 = 22{,}700{,}000$.'

The X axis range is set to the number of trading periods configured by the experimental settings. The recent 20-session movement is displayed by clicking on the 'Auto (X).' The number of periods can be adjusted by imputing the period index in the 'Period' textbox. A graph can also be displayed independently by clicking of the 'Separate Window' button.

### *1.6.6 Positions*

The past number of long and short positions is displayed. The divergence width between long position (blue line) and short position (redline) is to be the number of partial positions at that time. The following functions are similar with the 'Chart' tab: Auto (Y), Auto (X), Maximum, Minimum, Period, and Separate Window.

### *1.6.7 STDOUT*

Selecting this tab allows you to display information provided by a server or embedded agents. Output messages for each machine agent can be loaded. Self-produced Java programs can be installed in the U-Mart system, while this book does not particularly introduce any such programs. By confirming the messages output by such prgrams, you can check whether machine agents are operating properly.

### *1.6.8 Pull-Down Menu*

There is a pull-down menu displayed by selecting the 'Help' from the menu bar (Fig. 1.18). When the 'Tutorial' is selected, the tutorial slides are displayed in a separate window. These slides have been utilized when holding a lecture for U-Mart beginners at universities or international academic conferences. The slides give an explanation on using the trading terminal to conduct network experiments. The English version is displayed when selecting the tutorial from the English U-Mart system program (MarketSimulator_en.exe). Additionally, the DOC folder contains a PDF slide document. You may utilize this PDF file when using slides in a presentation form, like a lecture. This PDF file was created to provide a simple 30 minute explanation about operations and server connection. The latter part of this file includes explanations of description methods for each settings file, the particular system in futures trading, such as margin system and Mark-to-Market, and trading strategies.

Selecting the 'Download' from the menu allows you to access the U-Mart Project website (u-mart.org) through a default web browser. You can download the latest version of U-Mart system from this website. In addition, a variety of other information related to U-Mart, such as previous U-Mart experimental results, is also available. 'Bug Report' displays a window for sending messages.

**Fig. 1.18** Pull-Down Menu

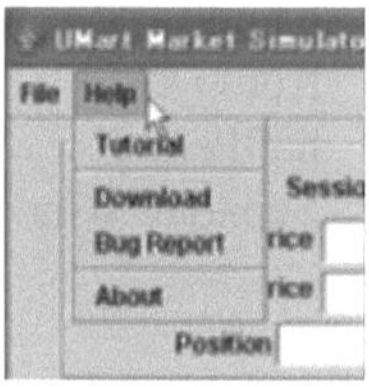

# Chapter 2
# How to Use the U-Mart System Network Edition

## 2.1 Introduction

Using the market simulator, chapter one introduced how to use one computer in order to deal with multiple machine agents preinstalled by default. The U-Mart system makes it possible for multiple agents to transact via a network. See the preface for the relation between the exchange and agents.

This chapter assumes that the trading terminal is used mainly by a human as an agent (trader) to make transactions in a computer-practice room in universities where multiple computers are connected to an available LAN. Conducting an actual trading experiment, this chapter introduces the flow from installing the market server that serves as an exchange to the consequential analysis.

## 2.2 Preparation

First, experimental equipment and the operational environment should be prepared. The U-Mart system is a platform-independent system since it has been developed in Java language. However, a server machine that serves to an exchange is required to handle a vast amount of orders from clients, which burdens the server heavily. Adequate performance and stable system environment are very essential.

### *2.2.1 Network Environment*

Experiments through a network require a server machine that serves as the exchange and multiple client machines as an agent. The market server is an application program serving as an exchange on the server machine, and the trading terminals serve as the agent in the client machines. These machines can communicate via TCP/IP, but recent computer practice rooms connected to the LAN are believed to meet the requirements.

### 2.2.2 Market Server Operation Environment

The market server is independent from the execution-platform since it has been developed in Java language. Operational checks have been conducted with Windows XP / 2000, Linux (i386) and MacOS X (PowerPC) on the U-Mart system contained in the attached CD-ROM. Especially convenient is that Java Runtime Environment (JRE) is also contained for the U-Mart systems for Windows and Linux, so the systems can be started with only the attached CD-ROM.[1] If your computer environment can operate the market simulator as related in Chapter 1, it likewise can operate the market server.

Confirm the specifications regarding the machine performance required. However, the machine load depends on the number of agents that are connecting, so a high-spec server machine is required to conduct such a large-scale experiment. Particularly, in connection with the operation on Java platform, a larger memory size is always better.

You can refer to the past results of transaction experiments with simultaneous connections that have been collected from 200 client computers simultaneously connected to the market server on a server machine (Pentium4 2.4GHz, 512MB RAM, Windows 2000). The number of simultaneous connections depends on the server machine's RAM and/or the network conditions.

Operation Specifications

*Windows XP/2000*

800MHz of Pentium3 processor, 512MB of system memory, and hard drive capacity of 256MB free space or more are required. The network connections are necessary for the server to communicate with client PCs via TCP/IP.

*Linux*

800MHz of Pentium3 processor, 512MB of system memory, and hard drive capacity of 256MB free space or more are required. X-Window (X11) environment is required to be installed for the GUI operation of the market server and trading terminal. The network connections are necessary for the server to communicate with client PCs via TCP/IP.

The operation check of the U-Mart system contained in the attached CD-ROM was conducted with FedoraCore 4/5 preinstalled by default.

---

[1] Java environment is preinstalled in MacOS X by default.

*MacOS X*

500MHz of PowerMac G4/G5 or more are required, and MacOS X version 10.3 or greater should be installed. The network connections are necessary for the server to communicate with client PCs via TCP/IP.

The operation check of the U-Mart system contained in the attached CD-ROM was conducted with MacOS X version 10.4.6/10.3.9 PowerPC edition.

### *2.2.3 Client PC Requirements*

A PC that serves as each agent is also needed. As a client, the trading terminal is used. Java Runtime Environment is included in the U-Mart systems for Windows and Linux, so the trading terminal can be operated on the same environment as that of the market simulator. There is no problem if the client's PC is using Windows XP/2000, Linux, and MacOS X, and being connected to the network to communicate with the server via TCP/IP.

## 2.3 Market Server Installation

*Windows*

Copy the UMartSystem-Windows folder (Fig. 2.1) in the attached CD-ROM to the hard drive of the server machine. Since the market server operation generates a vast amount of experimental results (logs), confirm whether the hard drive has sufficient free space.

If the experimental results are not saved, the market server can also be operated from the CD-ROM.

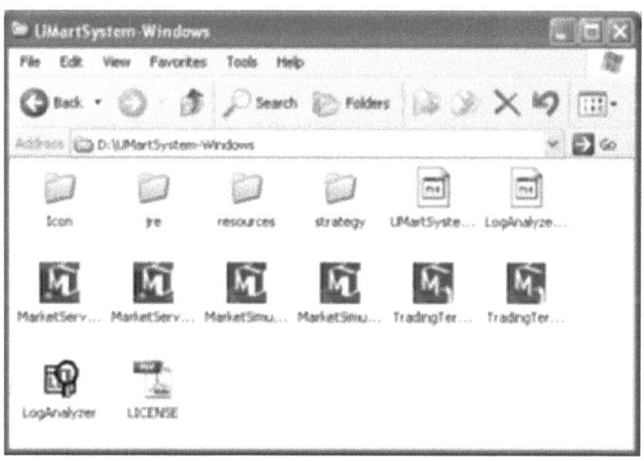


**Fig. 2.1** UMartSystem-Windows

*Linux*

Copy the UMartSystem-Linux.zip file contained in the attached CD-ROM to the hard drive in the server machine. Unzipping the copied file since this file is compressed in the ZIP format. The recent version of Linux provides GUI operation like Windows, which can decompress or copy such files by the GUI interface. Fig. 2.2 shows the example of the UMartSYstem-Linux folder after being decompressed by FedoraCore5.

Since the market server operation generates a vast amount of experimental results (logs), confirm whether the hard drive has sufficient free space.

Linux provides command operations to copy and decompress files. The following shows how to use the command prompt when the terminal is started to mount the CD-ROM and decompress the file after copying them under '/usr/local.'

```
% mount –t iso9660 /dev/cd/mnt/cd                    (Mount the CD)
% cp /mnt/cd/UMartSystem-Linux.zip/usr/local/        (Copy the file)
% unzip UMartSystem-Linux.zip                        (Unzip the file)
```

*MacOS X*

Copy the UMartSystem-Mac.zip file contained in the attached CD-ROM to the hard drive of the server. Unzip the file after copying it since this file is compressed in the ZIP format. MacOS X can unzip the compressed file in the ZIP format by double

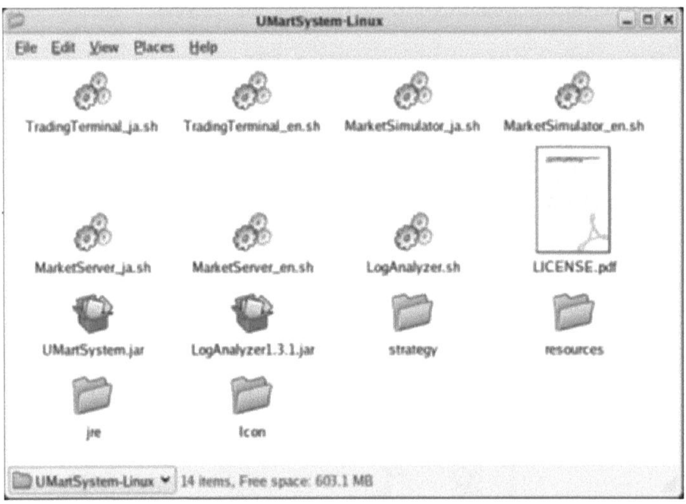


**Fig. 2.2** UMartSystem-Linux

clicking on it. Fig. 2.3 shows an example of the UMartSystem-Mac folder after unzipping.

Since MacOS X is a UNIX-based OS, starting the terminal provides the command prompt operation as in the case of Linux.

**Column: Client Installation**

Since the U-Mart system clients use the trading terminal contained in the UMartSystem folder, prepare a U-MartSystem folder on the hard drive in accordance with respective environments just as the case of the market server. If the market simulator was already operated, the trading terminal should also be installed in the same environment.

If the experimental results (logs) do not have to be saved, the trading terminal can be operated on the CD-ROM.

**Fig. 2.3** UMartSystem-Mac

## 2.4 Starting Market Server

### 2.4.1 How to Start

*Windows*

The UMartSystem-Windows folder contains two market servers – the Japanese version (MarketSerer_ja.exe) and the English version (MarketServer_en.exe). If the server is unable to display Japanese characters when using an English version of Windows, switch to the English version of the U-Mart server.

Double click on the MarketServer_ja.exe icon to start the Japanese version. After a short time, the U-Mart project logo is displayed, and then a dialogue box appears in order to configure settings such as trading-start time and various preset default values.

*Linux*

Where the GUI environment is available, the Japanese version of market server can be started by double clicking on the MarketServer_ja.sh icon just like in Windows. Double click on the MarketServer_en.sh icon when starting the English version.

When the program fails to start even by double clicking, you need to start the program by using the command prompt. In such a case, enter the following command after moving to the UMartSystem-Linux folder from the terminal, under the X-Window environment.

```
% ./MarketServer_ja.sh    [return]
```

Enter the following command when starting the English version of market server.

```
% ./MarketServer_en.sh    [return]
```

After the market server is started, the U-Mart logo is displayed just like in Windows, and then a dialogue box appears in order to configure settings such as trading-start time and various preset default values.

*MacOS X*

As with Windows, double click on the MarketServer_ja.app contained in the UmartSystem-Mac folder. The Japanese version of market server is started. Double click on the 'MarketServer_en.sh' icon when starting the English version.

In addition, as is the case of Linux, you can start the program by command prompt since MacOS X is a UNIX-based OS.

**Column: Starting the server with GUI on Windows/MacOS X**

In Windows or MacOS X, the U-Mart sever can be started with a command. After starting Command Prompt for Windows or Terminal for MacOS X, enter the command to start the server. Refer README.pdf contained in the attached CD-ROM for the details of the commands to be entered.

## *2.4.2 Experimental Environment Settings*

When starting the market server, the settings dialogue box as shown in Fig. 2.4 appears after the U-Mart project logo is displayed.

After setting each item, trading is begun by clicking on the 'OK' button. The detailed settings are configured with the configuration files (see paragraph 2.6). In this dialogue box, the file that registers experimental settings can be specified. Additionally, the basic experimental environment settings can be configured, such as trading experimental period, starting date, and the number of trading sessions per day.

Each setting item is described as follows.

Setting menu and File button This enables you to select the registered experimental environment (NickName). Clicking the 'File' button enables you to specify the file that registers the experimental settings. By default, TimeSeriesDefinitions.csv in the csv folder of the resources folder is specified.

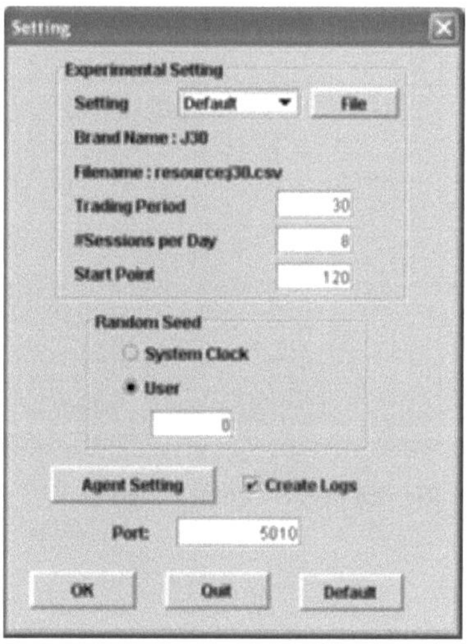


**Fig. 2.4** Environment Settings window

| | |
|---|---|
| Brand Name | Displays the name of the price time series, which is specified in the experimental configuration file. |
| Filename | Displays the filename of the price time series to be used. |
| Trading Period | Specifies the trading period of the experiment. |
| Sessions per Day | Specifies the number of trading sessions per day. |
| Start Point | Specifies the starting day of the price time series data. Enter the value of 120 or more. |
| Random Seed | Specifies the initial set value of random numbers that the system uses. Fixing the set value enables the user to obtain the experimental reproducibility. |
| Agent Setting button | Takes you to the setting window that configures human and machine agents used in the trading experiments (Fig. 2.5). |
| Create Logs | Experimental records are saved by checking this checkbox. |
| Port | Specifies the port number used in the network experiments. Number 5010 is specified by default. |
| OK button | The market server is started when this button is clicked (Fig. 2.6). |
| Quit button | The market server stops operating when this button is clicked. |
| Default button | Restore the default settings by clicking on this button. |

When clicking on the ‘OK’ button without changing any settings, the market server is started with the default settings, and waits for the connection to the client’s trading terminals.

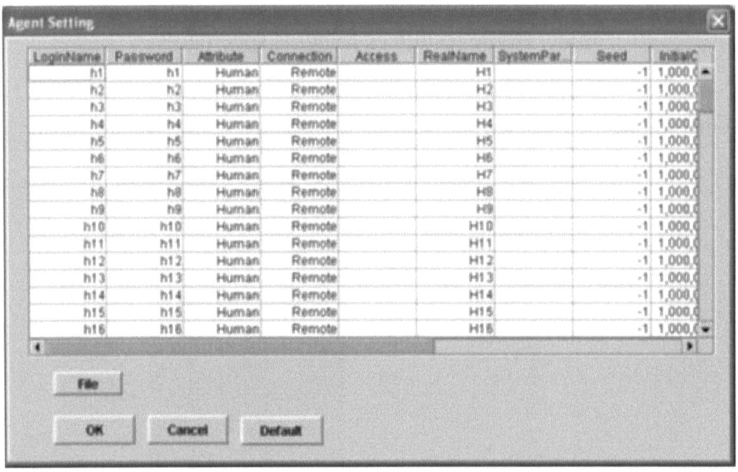


**Fig. 2.5** Agent Settings window

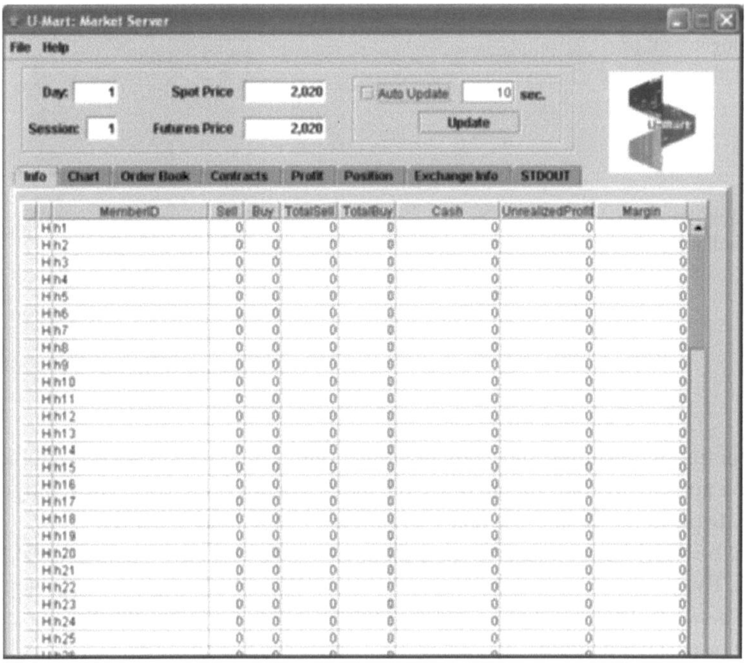


Fig. 2.6 Start window of market server

## 2.5 Trading Experiments

### *2.5.1 How to Connect to the Exchange Using a Trading Terminal*

Clients use the trading terminals. The Japanese and English versions are prepared for the trading terminals.

With Windows, as is the case with starting the market server, double click on 'TradingTerminal_ja.exe' for the Japanese version, and double click on 'TradingTerminal_en.exe' for the English version. The trading terminals for OSs other than Windows can also be started in the same way as starting the market server.

After the U-Mart project logo is displayed, the dialogue box that confirms the destination appears (Fig. 2.7). In this dialogue box, enter the IP address (hostname) and the port number of the computer running the market server. The default port number is 5010; however, sometimes the port number is changed when starting the market server.

When a wrong IP address (hostname) is entered or the market server is not ready, the following message is displayed: "Can not connect the server. Try again." In this case, reenter the right IP address (hostname), or try to reconnect once the market server has been started.

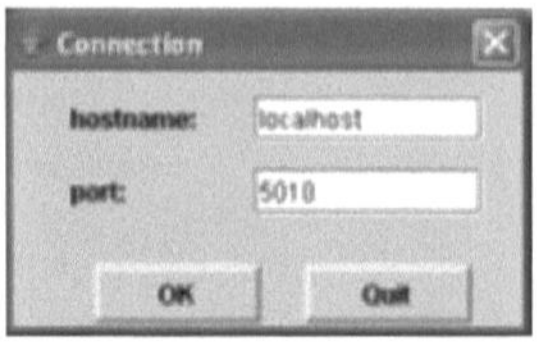


**Fig. 2.7** Destination confirmation dialogue box of trading terminal

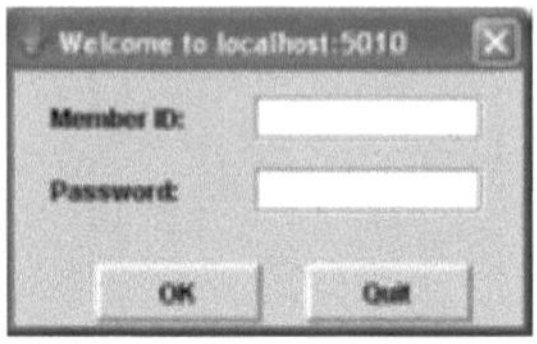


**Fig. 2.8** Trading terminal authentication dialogue box

When the trading terminal succeeds in connecting to the market server, another dialogue box appears to enter the member ID and password (Fig. 2.8). The dialogue box header displays the IP address and port number of the market server.

Click on the 'OK' button after entering the member ID and password assigned to each client. The password entered is not displayed. When entering a wrong member ID or password, the message is display that prompts you to reenter the correct member ID or password again.

**Column: Member ID and Password**

Member ID specifies an agent that participates in the transaction. The upper limit of agents possible to participate is determined by the configuration files. Since the number of agents also includes machine agents, notice that the member IDs of human agents cancel and overwrite machine agent's member IDs.

The member ID of an agent that has gone bankrupt is not available during the ongoing experiment. It is recommended to prepare in advance member IDs for those agents gone bankrupt so that they can come back to make transactions again.

The trading terminal starts successfully when it connects to the market server and actual transactions can be started if the market is open (Fig. 2.9).

The manner of operation after connecting to the market server is the same as the market simulation. The difference is that the 'STDOUT' tab displays only your information. The market server contains pieces of order information collected from multiple trading terminals; however, it is impossible for the trading terminal to col-

**Fig. 2.9** Trading terminal view

lect trading information other than your own. The trading terminal can collect common information from the market and the information about the agent himself.[2]

The actual transactions are conducted in the same manner as with using the market simulator. In the market simulator, the participants in transactions are only the embedded machine agents and 'you.' However, where the network server is used, it means that there are other agents participating in the transactions, other than 'you.'

Furthermore, when the transaction is made via the network, the trading terminal might suddenly crash or become unresponsive due to various difficulties that occur on the network. In such a case, where the market server is operating correctly, you can continue to participating in the transactions resuming at the previous point and with your trading information by restarting the trading terminal and reconnecting to the server again. However, where the trading terminal does not response because of bankruptcy, it is impossible to connect to the market server with the same member ID.

[2] The information an agent can display in the trading terminal can be controlled by each agent at the market server configuration files. For example, the trading terminal can divide the agents into two kinds, the agent that can display *Itayose* information and the agent that cannot do so.

### 2.5.2 Market Server Functions

From the market server side, when an agent logs on to the server, the green indicator on Member ID of the "Info" tab lights up to show which member ID is logged on.(Fig. 2.10). If the market server is running, you can log into the server even before the transactions start.

The market server is able to control the progression of market transaction. Checking the 'Auto Update' checkbox allows the making transactions in the specified time interval (by seconds). The transactions can be progressed manually by clicking on the 'Update' button.

There are only two ways to start a transaction. One is to activate the automatic update function checking the 'Auto Update' checkbox with the time interval specified. The other one is to progress the transaction manually by clicking the 'Update' button. The transactions do not progress unless you click on the 'Update' button when it is controlled manually. On the other hand, when the automatic update function works, the transaction can be paused temporarily by unchecking the 'Auto Update.'

During transactions, as is the case with the market simulator, the market server can display a variety of information, such as charts, market conditions, such as the order book, contract information of each agent, and profit and position information.

The following information can be displayed by the market server.

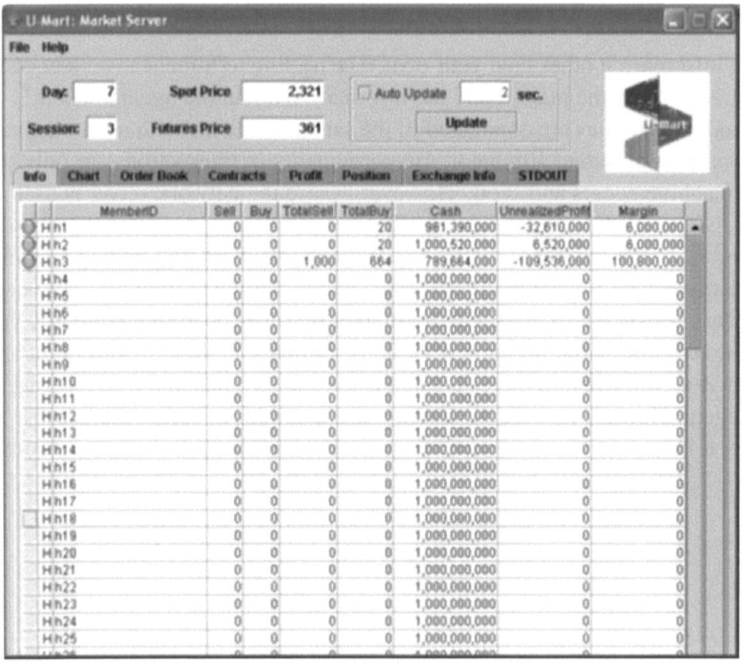

Fig. 2.10 Info-tab view of the market server

| | |
|---|---|
| Info | Displays the information about the agent currently logged on. The green indicator lights up when an agent is connected, and the red indicator lights up when an agent has gone into bankruptcy. In addition, a list of buy and sell information and asset information of each agent is displayed. |
| Chart | Displays the transition of spot price and futures price. |
| Order Book | Displays the present board information and the board graph of previous pricing. |
| Contracts Information | Displays the contract information of each of agents. |
| Profit | Displays the graph of agent-specific profit transition. |
| Position | Displays the graph of agent-specific positions transition. |
| Exchange Info | Displays the IP address and port number of the market server. |
| STDOUT | Displays the information of each agent recorded in log files. |

### *2.5.3 Transaction Experiment Termination*

How to quit the market server

The transaction results are recorded as logs if the 'Create Logs' checkbox was checked when starting the market server.

As is the case of creating logs with the market simulator, logs are saved as the CSV format file in the "UMARTxxxxxx (the executed date and time on the millisecond time scale are entered in 'xxxxxx' part)" folder, which is created in the same hierarchy location of the market server.[3] With these log files, more detailed analysis can be conducted easily by utilizing Log Analyzer that will be mentioned later, or by loading the log files into spreadsheet software like Microsoft Excel.

In the 'Session' textbox of the market server, the mark '-' is entered at the close of each transaction period (Fig. 2.11).

When selecting 'Quit' from File menu on the menu bar, a confirmation message appears. You can quit the market server by clicking on the 'OK' button. However, notice that if you quit the market server before logging off the trading terminals, the trading terminals will not operate (the terminals get hung-up) which prevents the clients from performing such operations as saving transaction logs. It is advisable for trading terminals to be logged off before quitting the market server.

[3] In MacOS X, where starting the market server by double clicking from GUI, the log folder is created in the root directory (usually, Macintosh HD:). Notice that it causes an error depending on user's authority. When starting the market server from the command prompt, the log folder is created in the same hierarchy with the market server.

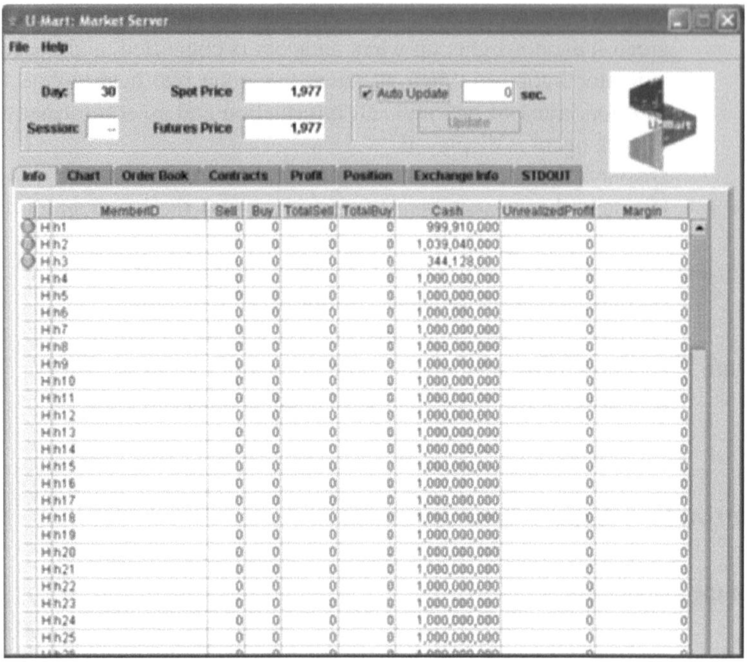


Fig. 2.11 Display of the market server at close of transaction

How to quit the trading terminal

After closing your transactions, you can quit directly or select to save the transaction records (logs, Fig. 2.12). To save your own transaction results, select 'Save' from File menu. The window comes up to save logs (Fig. 2.13).

Specifying the filename to save here, your transaction results are saved in four CSV files (***_order.csv, ***_posisiont.csv, ***_price.csv, ***_profit.csv). Fig. 2.14 shows the example of the files that are created with the filename 'Test' specified.

Fig. 2.12 Saved Market Server's logs

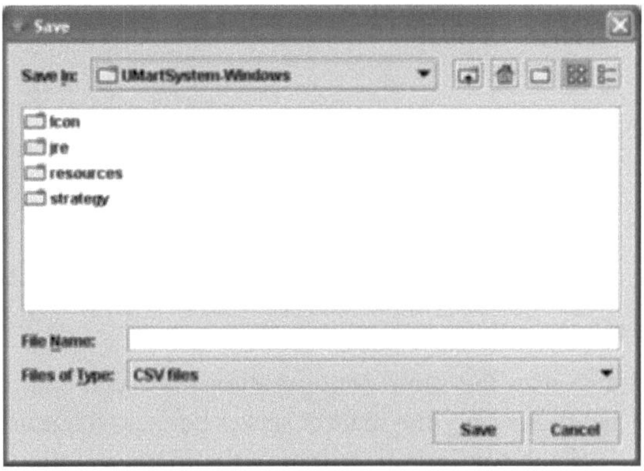


**Fig. 2.13** Save window of your trading logs

**Fig. 2.14** Saved CSV files

To quit the trading terminal, select 'Quit' from File menu. Then, the final results of all the agents who participated in this transaction are displayed (Fig. 2.15). You can confirm the final results by selecting 'Cancel' here, and your transaction results and others can be compared. Click on the 'OK' button to exit viewing the final results.

To quit the trading terminal, select the 'Quit' from the File menu once again. By clicking on the 'OK' button after the confirmation message appears, you can quit the trading terminal.

## 2.6 Configuration Files

The configuration files are contained in the csv folder (Fig. 2.16), under the 'resources' placed in the UmartSystem-Windows folder.[4] Since the market simulator

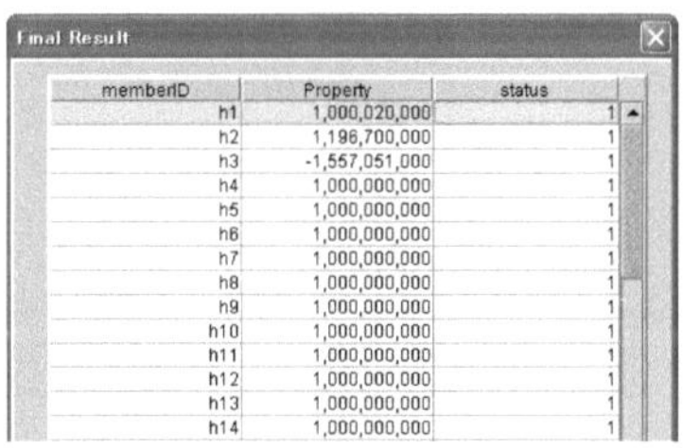

| memberID | Property | status |
|---|---|---|
| h1 | 1,000,020,000 | 1 |
| h2 | 1,196,700,000 | 1 |
| h3 | -1,557,051,000 | 1 |
| h4 | 1,000,000,000 | 1 |
| h5 | 1,000,000,000 | 1 |
| h6 | 1,000,000,000 | 1 |
| h7 | 1,000,000,000 | 1 |
| h8 | 1,000,000,000 | 1 |
| h9 | 1,000,000,000 | 1 |
| h10 | 1,000,000,000 | 1 |
| h11 | 1,000,000,000 | 1 |
| h12 | 1,000,000,000 | 1 |
| h13 | 1,000,000,000 | 1 |
| h14 | 1,000,000,000 | 1 |

**Fig. 2.15** Final results

[4] 'resources' is placed in the UMartSystem-Linux folder for Linux, and in the UMartSystem-Mac folder for MacOS X.

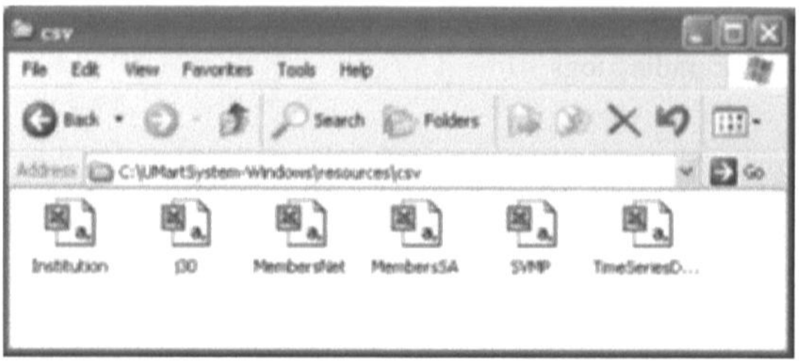


**Fig. 2.16** csv folder in 'resources'

also uses the same configuration files, you can refer the following information for using not only the market server but also the market simulator.

Each configuration item of the file is as follows.

Institution.csv — Player system configuration in the market simulator. See agent's settings part for each configuration item.

J30.csv — Default time series data.

TimeSeriesDefinitions.csv — Time series configuration that is used in the experiments and experimental condition settings.

MembersSA.csv — Each setting of machine agents that are embedded in the market simulator by default.

MembersNet.csv — Each setting of agents that participate in transaction experiments conducted by the market server.

SVMP.csv — Connection settings between the exchange and agents. No need to change usually.

### *2.6.1 Time Series Configurations (j30.csv)*

The U-Mart system is futures market, so the actual time series data should be provided in advance. As default time series data that the market server and the market simulator use, the past J30 stock index data provided by Mainichi Shimbun is prepared as j30.csv (Table 2.1).

Date — '0' is entered. The date is output to the logs after the transaction experiments.

**Table 2.1** j30.csv

| Date | Session | SpotPrice | FuturePrice |
|---|---|---|---|
| 0 | 0 | 2750 | −1 |
| 0 | 0 | 2800 | −1 |
| ⋮ | ⋮ | ⋮ | ⋮ |

Session — '0' is entered. The session number of each date is output to the logs after the transaction experiments.

SpotPrice — Spot price time series to be used when the transaction experiments are entered.

FuturePrice — Future price time series is entered. '-1' is entered when a price is not determined.

### 2.6.2 *Configuration of Experimental Conditions (TimeSeriesDefinitions.csv)*

Preparing a number of experimental settings with time series data, trading period, trading volume per a day (the number of sessions) and a start day of time series specified, each set of experimental condition can be named (with NickName) as experimental settings. This will allow the user to select experimental conditions when a transaction experiment is to be conducted (Table 2.2).

NickNames, as experimental settings, are displayed and can be selected from the 'Setting' form of the initial configuration dialogue when the market server is started. When it comes to the trading period, trading volume per a day (the number of sessions), and starting day of time series, these can be changed after selecting the desired NickName.

NickName — The experimental name given to experimental settings specified. When conducting various experiments, each experiment can be distinguished according to the different "NickName."

Filename — The time series data that an experiment uses is specified. Where using j30.csv in the csv folder placed in the 'resources' folder, specify like the following: "resource:j30.csv." When preparing a time series data in the same hierarchy of the market server, the time series file path is set by specifying it as the following: "file:***.csv."

BrandName — The name of price time series data is specified. J30 does not have to be changed.

StartStep — The start day of price time series data is specified. Enter the value of 120 or more.

**Table 2.2** TimeSeriesDefinitions.csv

| NickName | Filename | BrandName | StartStep | MaxDate | NoOfSessionsPerDay |
|---|---|---|---|---|---|
| Default | resource:j30.csv | J30 | 120 | 30 | 8 |
| EX1 | resource:j30.csv | J30 | 340 | 20 | 4 |
| ⋮ | ⋮ | ⋮ | ⋮ | ⋮ | ⋮ |

| | |
|---|---|
| MaxDate | The number of days for transaction experiments is specified. |
| NoOfSessionsPerDay | The trading volume per a day (the number of sessions) is specified. |

## *2.6.3 Agent Settings (MembersSA.csv, MembersNet.csv, Institution.csv)*

The following two csv files configure the agents that participate in a transaction: MembersSA.scv for the market simulator and MemebersNet.csv for the market server (Table 2.3). These two csv files have the similar formats but different parameter settings. Many configuration items have been prepared, however, the items required to conduct transaction experiments on the network are limited.

Additionally, you can confirm the agent settings loaded by clicking on the 'Agent Setting' button on the initial settings dialogue box. Furthermore, you can also specify another agent's settings file.

| | |
|---|---|
| LoginName | The user ID of an agent logs in is specified. |
| Password | The password is specified. |
| Attribute | Agent attributes ('Human' for a human agent, 'Machine' for a machine agent) are specified. |
| Connection | Agent connection methods ('Remote' for a network connection, 'Local' for a local connection) are specified. |
| Access | Controls information presented to each agent ('CHART' for a chart, 'BOARD' for the order book, 'ORDER' for a current order, 'ORDER_RESULT' for contract information, 'PROFIT' for a profit, 'POSITION' for a position, 'STDOUT' for standard output). The information which an agent does not want to display is listed. Separate each name with colons (:) in order to specify several names. Since the item 'Access' is blank by default, all information is presented to agents. |

**Table 2.3** MembersNet.csv

| LoginName | Password | Attribute | Connection | Access | RealName | System Parameters | ··· |
|---|---|---|---|---|---|---|---|
| h1 | h1 | Human | Remote | | h1 | | ··· |
| h2 | h2 | Human | Remote | | h2 | | ··· |
| ⋮ | ⋮ | ⋮ | ⋮ | ⋮ | ⋮ | | |
| TrendStrategy | passwd2 | Machine | Local | | Strategy.TrendStrategy | WidthOfPrice=10 | ··· |
| ⋮ | ⋮ | ⋮ | ⋮ | ⋮ | ⋮ | ⋮ | ⋮ |

RealName Specifies a real agent name. The real agent name is specified in the case of network connection, and the program name (class file) of machine agent is specified in the case of local connection. For example, when specifying the 'TrandStrategy.class' file in the strategy folder, enter as 'strategy.TrandStrategy.'

SystemParameters The initial setting values of each machine agent under the local connection are specified. When specifying multiple settings, separate each setting name with colons (:). See the appendix regarding the initial setting for the machine agents embedded.

Seed The initial setting values are specified in order to randomly specify the machine agents used under a local connection.

InitialCash Initial retention asset. One billion yen by default.

TradingUnit One unit for an order. 1,000 units by default.

FeePerUnit Exchange fee. 0 yen by default.

MarginRate Deposit (margin) money. 30,000 yen per one unit by default.

MaxLoan The upper threshold of exchange debt when going bankruptcy. 30 million yen by default.

Interest The interest rate of exchange debt. 10 percent by default.

These settings can be configured according to each individual agent. For example, the transaction experiment among agents having different initial retention assets can be easily conducted. Additionally, it is possible to conduct a transaction experiment to confirm to differences between transactions, in which order book information is available and is not available.

## 2.7 Analyzing Log Files

After experiments using the U-Mart system, the logs that record the transaction details remain. The trading terminal leaves only the logs related to an agent's transaction. On the other hand, the logs recorded with the market server and market simulator contain all the transactions made by agents, so it takes considerable time to analyze those logs. For this reason, the program called 'Log Analyzer' is prepared in order to take extract particular agent's information.

### *2.7.1 Log Analyzer*

Log Analyzer is an application program that graphically displays the transaction history of the entire market and the buy-and-sell history of the agents, This information can be loaded from the log folder created when quitting the U-Mart. Using Log Analyzer allows displaying the buy-and-sell results of each agent visually. Moreover, starting multiple Log Analyzers display the buy-and-sell results graphs among all

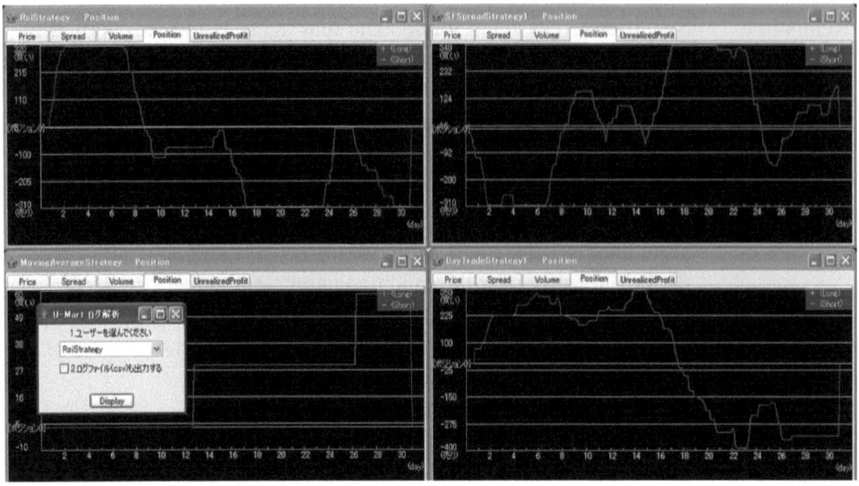


**Fig. 2.17** Starting multiple Log Analyzers (Japanese Version)

or some of the agents in order to compare and analyze them (Fig. 2.17). Detailed numerical data can be outputted in csv files.

## *2.7.2 How to Use Log Analyzer*

The use of Log Analyzer is common to the logs of trading terminal, market server, and market simulator.

1. Double click on 'LogAnalyzer.exe'.[5]
2. The folder 'UMARTxxxxxx' (the executed date and time on the millisecond time scale are entered in 'xxxxxx' part) is created in UMartSystem folder at the close of game, select this folder (Fig. 2.18). In the case of the market simulator, the 'Create Log' checkbox of the 'Setting' dialogue box is unchecked at the start of a session. Notice this checkbox should be checked before starting an experiment.
3. Right-click on 'Open' after selecting the appropriate log folder, then the 'U-Mart Log Analyzer' dialogue box appears (Fig. 2.19). Select the user that you want to display from the pull down menu of '1.' Check the checkbox of '2' if detailed buy-and-sell data of the selected agent is needed to be output in a CSV file (The file will be output with the filename " 'agent name'_log.csv"). Click on the 'Display' button after selecting the agent.
4. Each window is displayed graphically. Multiple agents can be displayed simultaneously by starting multiple Log Analyzers, and the windows that are displayed can be zoomed in and out by changing the window size.

[5] Double click on 'LogAnalyzer.sh' for Linux, and on 'LogAnalyzer.app' for MacOS X.

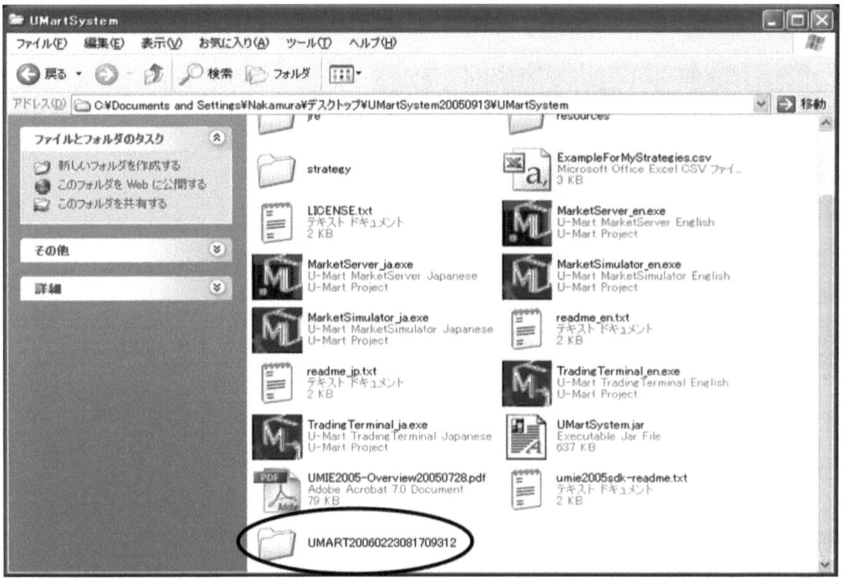


**Fig. 2.18** Selecting the folder (Japanese Version)

**Fig. 2.19** Start Dialogue Box (Japanese Version)

## *2.7.3 Display Contents*

In Log Analyzer, the displayed contents can be switched by selecting the tabs. The ‘Price,’ ‘Spread,’ and ‘Volume’ tabs display the entire market results, so the common results are displayed by selecting any of these tabs. The ‘Position’ and ‘Unrealized-Profit’ tabs display the results of each agent.

*1. Price tab (Fig. 2.20)*

Displays the time series of spot and futures prices. The spot price is prepared by the server, whereas futures price is produced as a result of the transaction made by agents.

*2. Spread tab (Fig. 2.21)*

Displays the price difference (spread) between spot price and futures price with bar graphs. This tab is useful when evaluating the arbitrage transaction strategy to

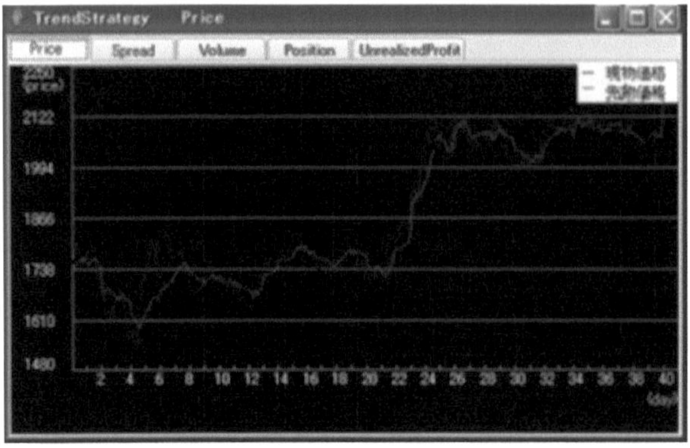


Fig. 2.20 Price tab (Japanese Version)

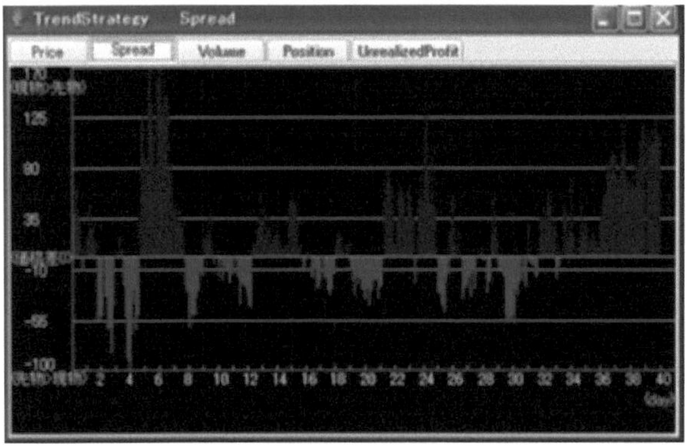


Fig. 2.21 Spread tab (Japanese Version)

determine to buy or sell with a price spread. It is possible to confirm whether you could enter a timely trade at a point of significant price discrepancy by using the arbitrage transaction strategy. In addition, you could evaluate whether you could close the positions when the price divergence dwindles in order to establish a profit.

3. *Volume tab (Fig. 2.22)*

Displays the contracted volume (trading turnover) of each session.

4. *Position tab (Fig. 2.23)*

Display user's positions (how many short position and long position the user has). In the trend strategy, it should be confirmed that the long position is increased as the price rises. With position transition, you can analyze whether you are alert by maintaining a good balance in positions, or taking risk preferences by being extreme in positions. Notice that the value on the graph returned to the location of '0' since

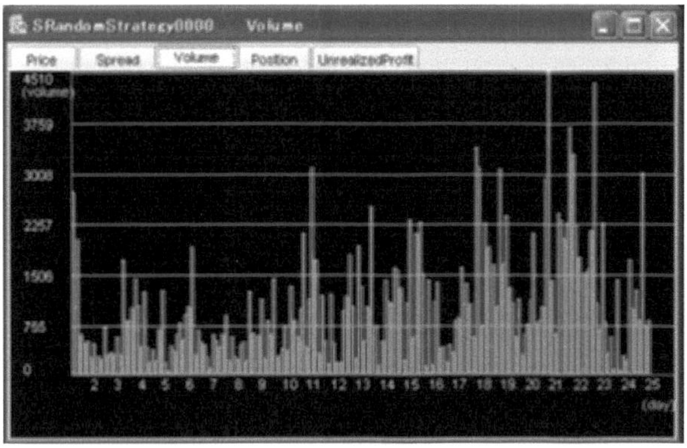


**Fig. 2.22** Volume tab (Japanese Version)

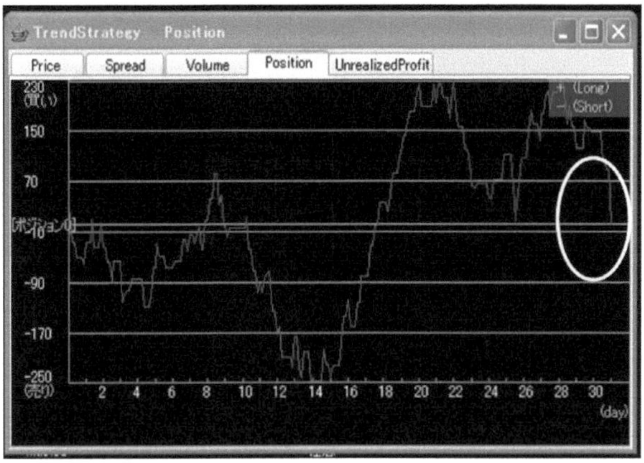


**Fig. 2.23** Position tab (Japanese Version)

the positions that are carried over will be forced into settlement after the end of the final day transactions (the circle in Fig. 2.23).

*5. Unrealized Profit tab (Fig. 2.24)*

Displays the transition of user's unrealized profit and loss. In the U-Mart specifications, unrealized profit and loss are updated not after each session but each day, so this tab displays the transition of unrealized profit and loss day by day. The green bar in the graph indicates the final profit and loss after conducting Mark-to-Market on the positions carried over (the circle in Fig. 2.24). Where the transaction ends with a large amount of positions carried over, notice that the positions are forced into settlement at the final spot price and the results vary significantly.

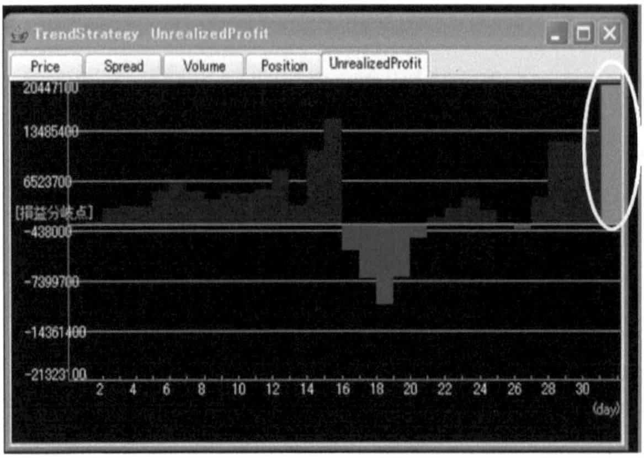


**Fig. 2.24** Unrealized Profit tab (Japanese Version)

# Chapter 3
# Futures Market and U-Mart Experiment

## 3.1 Introduction

The U-Mart is a virtual futures trading system. This chapter gives a description of the following preliminary knowledge required to understand and enjoy U-Mart: 1) Futures market mechanism, 2) Stock-index futures mechanism, 3) U-Mart system overview, and 4) Stock price prediction.[1]

Futures markets in Japan have a long history, and originate with *Choai-mai* rice trading (rice trading with an account book) conducted in Osaka during the Edo period. From back then, price forecasting using ruled line was likely popular. With such a background, Japanese futures trading terms are difficult to understand because those terms include original old Japanese words, English words translated into Japanese, and English words written in Japanese *Katakana*. See the glossary at the close of this chapter as necessary.

## 3.2 Futures Market

### *3.2.1 Futures Market Mechanism*

Exchange

The exchange system has been established in order to deal with price decision and transaction promptly in high volume. However, there is a significant difference between the commodities we handle in our daily lives and what the commodities exchanges handle (currencies or bonds).

---

[1] This chapter has been added and altered on [10], which had been prepared as a text book of the U-Mart workshop held in Osaka City University on $17^{th}$ of May, 2001. Section 3.2.1 and 3.3 referred [22] and [23], section 3.5 referred [8], and section 3.4 referred [2], respectively. Additionally, authoring the entire chapter, [25] was significantly referred to.

The transaction objects handled by exchanges include the following things: currencies such as the Dollar and Euro, stocks and bonds, cereals like wheat and soybeans, fuel such as oil and coal, industrial materials such as ironstone and rubber. The following characteristics can be observed in these transaction objects.

(1) Homogeneous
(2) Quantities that can finely be measured
(3) Existing in huge numbers
(4) Easy to store
(5) Easy to resell (used commodities that do not fall in price)

In economics, these qualities are referred to as "high liquidity."

Additionally, almost all commodities we buy in stores have fixed prices. Only the sellers have the right to change the prices, however, the prices are not frequently changed. Furthermore, at the moment of a transaction, the seller (store) and the buyer (the individual) have one-on-one relationship. On the other hand, when transactions made at exchanges, a number of sellers and buyers participate in the transaction simultaneously, and the prices vary constantly depending on the condition of supply and demand.

Usually, only the members who pay the membership fee are able to participate in transaction on the exchange. In addition, the members must pass a rigorous screening. This is because the exchange's maintenance, operation, and employment costs – can be regarded as the price formation costs – these are immeasurable and the membership fee is devoted to cover these costs. In addition, since the unit price of buying and selling of the transaction are significant, such a rigorous screening is needed to prevent untrustworthy people from participating in the transaction.

### Definition of Futures Trading

Exchange transactions consist of the following three aspects:

(1) Agreement (to decide to conduct buying and selling)
(2) Delivery (deliver the commodities or bonds from a seller to buyer)
(3) Settlement (handling of money)

The transaction conducting the above aspects simultaneously is called spot trading. In futures trading, just the agreement is made at present time; delivery and settlement are conducted at a future date.

More specifically, futures trading is a transaction that a seller and buyer undertake to turn over a certain product at a given future due date, with the price determined at present time (this is called 'contracted') (Fig. 3.1). The price and volume are determined at present time, whereas the product does not move until the settlement date. Actually, the product is not delivered from the seller to buyer because netting is taken place after conducting the closed trade by the due date (netting and the closed trade will be mentioned later).

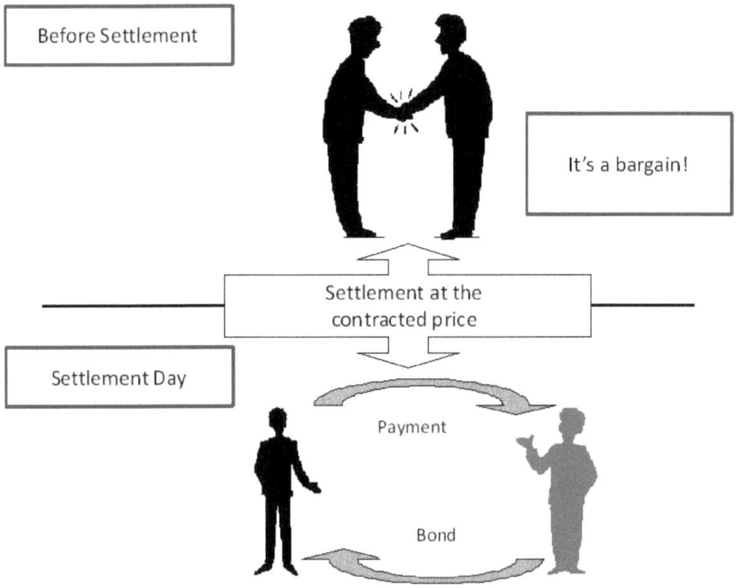


**Fig. 3.1** Futures Market Mechanism

The ‘products’ mentioned here do not include only commodities such as serials like rice or red beans, precious metals like gold and silver, and oil, or rubber. It also includes financial commodities such as stocks and national bonds, in addition to foreign currencies such as the Dollar and Euro. Moreover, such a commodity categorized as information like stock index handled in U-Mart can be included as a product.

## *3.2.2 Futures Market Functions*

Futures markets have a variety of functions. The functions of futures market discussed in [13] are introduced as follows.

Risk aversion (Hedging function)

Futures trading has the function that averts (hedges) the price volatility risk. Now, let the example of a company[2] that deals with foreign companies to explain this function (Fig. 3.2). Let's suppose, a company (Company A) exports a product worth

[2] Usually, the futures products in foreign exchange market is called ‘exchange reservation.’

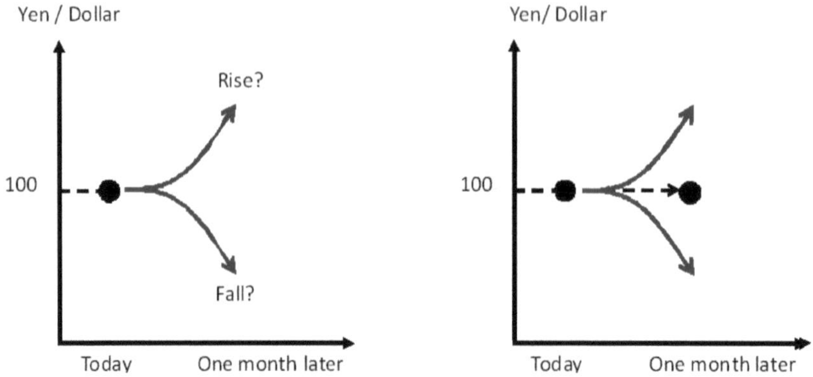


**Fig. 3.2** Merchandise transaction of a company

$10,000 to the United States, and is to receive the income one month later. In this case present exchange rate is 100 yen to the dollar.

In this case, Company A waits for the exchange price concerning how it varies during the next month while being kept in suspense; on the other hand, the company has a demand for establishing the income. Here, Company A sells the futures product of 10,000 dollars' worth that has the contract month of next month with an exchange rate of 100 yen to the dollar. By doing so, Company A is able to avert the price volatility risk. Similarly, if Company A imports commodity of worth $10,000, Company A can avert the risk by buying a futures product.

Where Company A has already purchased a futures product, even if the dollar gets weaker and the yen gets strong one month later with rate of 95 yen to the dollar, Company A can prevent suffering a loss because the profit was established with a 100 yen to the dollar rate. Conversely, if the dollar gets strong and the yen gets weaken with a 105 yen to the dollar, Company A cannot make a profit (Fig. 3.3).

Suchlike transaction, namely, clearing the past orders by placing the buying order (selling) for the past selling (buying) order is called a closed trade. Additionally, the

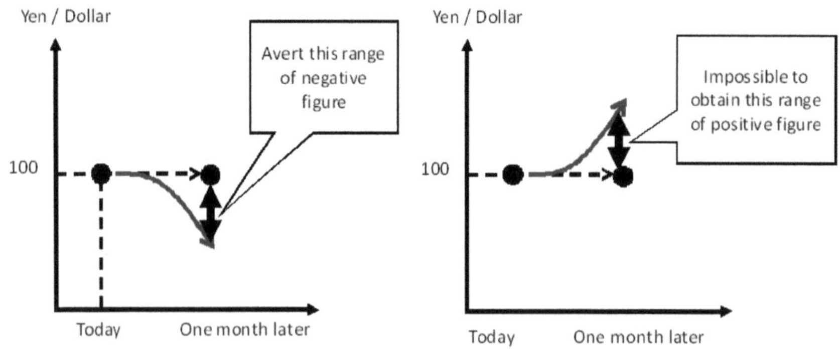


**Fig. 3.3** Merchandise transaction of a company

transaction to connect selling and buying is called hedge trading (hedging). For this reason, averting the risk with hedge trading is referred to as risk hedge.

Standardization function of relative price

Relative price difference of futures market tends to be standardized by arbitrage transaction (arbitrage trading) using the price difference between the spot market and futures market. Hence, the futures market and spot market having different contract months are traded on exchanges; however, the spot price and futures price do not deviate significantly.

Suppose that the following prices are the current delivery price (futures product settled current month) and two-month delivery price (futures product settled next month) of a certain commodity today.

- Current delivery price: 12,000 yen
- Two-month delivery price: 10,000 yen

Here, one trader predicts that the two-month delivery price will rise by 1,000 yen within the current month because the two-month price is greatly cheaper than the current delivery price. In this case, he will take the following actions.

- Sell 100 units of the current delivery price of 12,000 yen
- Buy 120 units of the two-month delivery price of 11,000 yen

Since this buying and selling is the pairing of the sell order of 1,200,000 yen and buy order of 1,200,000 yen, the trader does not suffer any loss. A few days later, the two-month delivery price turned into 11,000 yen as he expected, so he bought back 100 units of current delivery and sold 120 units of two-month delivery.

- Buy 100 units of the current delivery price of 12,000 yen
- Sell 120 units of the two-month delivery price of 11,000 yen

With this buying and selling, the marginal advantage of 120,000 yen worth is generated. By means of such *arbitrage procedures*, the two-month delivery price rises by contined buying and the current delivery price falls by continued selling. In other words, the relative price is standardized by futures trading.

Function of increasing the volume of actual product distribution

Even if the actual product distribution stops because of a significant difference between the demand price and supply price in the spot market, there is the possibility that the actual product demand price and the selling for speculation purpose corresponds well together due to the existence of futures market where speculation and hedging is conducted. Additionally, when short selling has taken place in the futures market, the actual product should be provided. Hence, out of necessity, the demand comes into request, and there is a possibility that a part of the demand uses the real market. The trader suffers loss in this case; however, the distribution volume of real products increases as a result of the loss.

### 3.2.3 Classification of Futures Market Participants

From the viewpoint of 'Market Microstructure Theory' [15, 16], let us classify the market participants in accord with their reasons for participating in the market.

Taken socially, the reason why a future trading is needed is because of "relocation and aversion to the price volatility risk." The people who utilize futures markets desire to avert the price volatility until the due date, and try to establish the delivery and payment price of the present time. These people who participate in the market with such a reason are referred to as a 'hedger.'

Of the people who participate in the markets; there are two different types other than hedgers. One is a trader who predicts the change in a future price and aims at the profit with its prediction, known as a speculator. The speculator serves to establish the transaction that cannot be made by only hedgers, increasing the sales volume of the market.

The other one tries to use the profit margins of the price difference among markets such as the Tokyo Stock Exchange or the Osaka Securities Exchange. This trader type is referred to as an 'arbitrager.' When U-Mart is progressed parallel with the actual real market in accord with real-time, it can also be considered that the U-Mart participants conduct buying and selling in the actual real market. With high awareness of U-Mart, those traders who try to trade actual products referring to U-Mart might appear in principle; however, this is not of much practical thought.

In U-Mart, the hedgers and arbitragers do not appear. All the participants participate in U-Mart as speculators.

### 3.2.4 Settlement System in Futures Market

The settlement system which is also a characteristic of futures market has period between the agreement and settlement.

#### Mark-to-Market and unrealized profit and loss

The result of futures trading is not known until the due date, whether it results finally in negative or positive value. However, you can calculate whether you will sustain a loss or make a profit if the due date comes and the price remained the same as that of the present day.

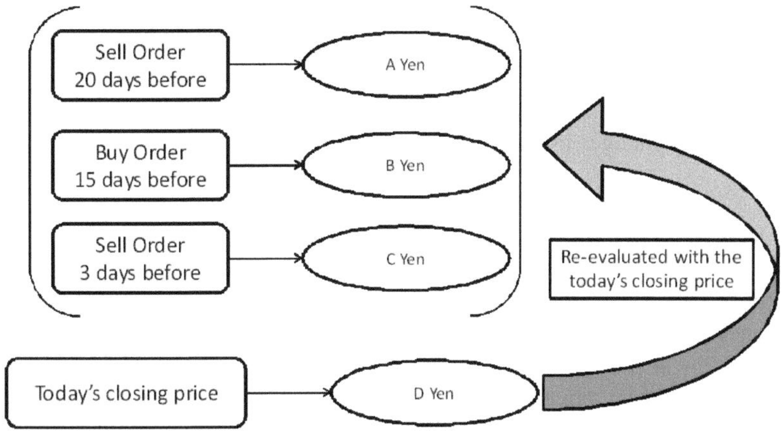


**Fig. 3.4** Mark-to-Market

The exchange reevaluates the past buying and selling orders placed by each market participant with the present day price, and calculates how much loss sustained or how much profit made from daily price volatility. This is referred to as Mark-to-Market (Fig. 3.4).

The profit and loss coming out as a result of Mark-to-Market is referred to as an unrealized profit and loss. The expression 'unrealized' used here means that 'the price is not established until netting has taken place in the contract month.' Actually, the unrealized profit and loss increases and decreases accompanied by the increase and decrease of prices (see the sample calculation below).

Sample calculation of Mark-to-Market and unrealized profit and loss

Suppose, the closing price today of futures price is 1,070 yen, and the transactions shown in Table 3.1 are made up to today.

The unrealized profit and loss at today is 50,000 yen, according to the following calculation: $\{(1,070-1,020)\times 10,000\}+\{(1,050-1,070)\times 5,000\}+\{(1,070-1,100)\times 5,000\}=50,000.$[3]

**Table 3.1** Example of Mark-to-Market (1)

| date | buy/sell | trading price (JPY) | trading volume (unit) |
|---|---|---|---|
| 3 days before | buy | 1,020 yen | 10,000 |
| 10 days before | sell | 1,050 yen | 5,000 |
| 12 days before | buy | 1,100 yen | 5,000 |

[3] Since the unrealized profit and loss is "the profit (loss) generated by price volatility at buying (selling)," the calculation will be 'the present day price - the price bought' in the case of buying

If the futures price rises by 1,100 yen the next day, the unrealized profit and loss will be 65,000 yen. Conversely, if the futures price falls to 1,000 yen, the unrealized profit and loss will be a loss of 450,000 yen (the calculation method is the same, try once doing by it yourself). As just described, the unrealized profit and loss varies depending on the changes in futures prices.

Where the unrealized profit and loss do not change

When positions are zero, the unrealized profit and loss is not influenced by Mark-to-Market. The unrealized profit and loss is always constant even though the price changes. Let the next example explain this.

Suppose, the closing price today of future price is 1,120 yen, and the past transaction history is shown in Table 3.2.

In this case, the unrealized profit and loss will be 800,000, which means a profit of 800,000 yen, with the following calculation: $\{(1,120-1,050)\times 10,000\}+\{(1,100-1,120)\times 5,000\}+\{(1,160-1,120)\times 5,000\}=800,000$.

Where the futures price rises from 1,120 to 1,150 yen, the unrealized profit and loss will be 800,000 yen with the following calculation: $\{(1,150-1,050)\times 10,000\}+\{(1,100-1,150)\times 5,000\}+\{(1,160-1,150)\times 5,000\}=800,000$. Additionally, where the futures price falls to 1,000 yen, the unrealized profit and loss will also be 800,000 yen with the following calculation: $\{(1,000-1,050)\times 10,000\}+\{(1,100-1,000)\times 5,000\}+\{(1,160-1,000)\times 5,000\}=800,000$. As shown above, the unrealized profit and loss is established where positions are zero.

The unrealized profit and loss by means of past buying and selling can be divided into the following two parts:

1. The part that is already established as a result of offsetting of buying and selling.
2. The part of selling on balance (buying on balance) that remains as a result of offsetting.

**Table 3.2** Example of Mark-to-Market (2)

| date | buy/sell | trading price (JPY) | trading volume (unit) |
|---|---|---|---|
| 7 days before | buy | 1,050 yen | 10,000 |
| 10 days before | sell | 1,100 yen | 5,000 |
| 15 days before | sell | 1,160 yen | 5,000 |

order (it is not the day of buying, but how much profit could be gained if buying today). In the case of selling order, the calculation will be 'the price sold - the present day price' (it is not the day of selling, but how much profit could be gained if selling today). The prices are switched before and after the minus (-) mark depending on the buy or sell order, so the calculation should be done with care.

The unrealized profit and loss that corresponds to part 1 is absolutely put into practice when the contract month comes. Only part 2 is influenced by Mark-to-Market and price volatility.

Positions and netting

The contracted orders are called a 'contract (open interest)' in the futures market, and the contracts (buying, selling and its volume) by each member has are called 'positions.' Where long contracts exceed short contracts, it is known as 'having long positions,' and vice versa 'having short positions'. In addition, the difference between short contracts and long contracts is referred to as 'trade balance contract.' When saying 'position', it merely indicates the trade balance contract.

In the futures markets, the transactions are settled in a lump sum in the contract month (settlement day).[4] Since the trade prices of each transaction that has been made different respectively until the contract month, traders receive (or pay) the price, worth the difference of each trade price. This is called 'netting.' (Fig. 3.5)

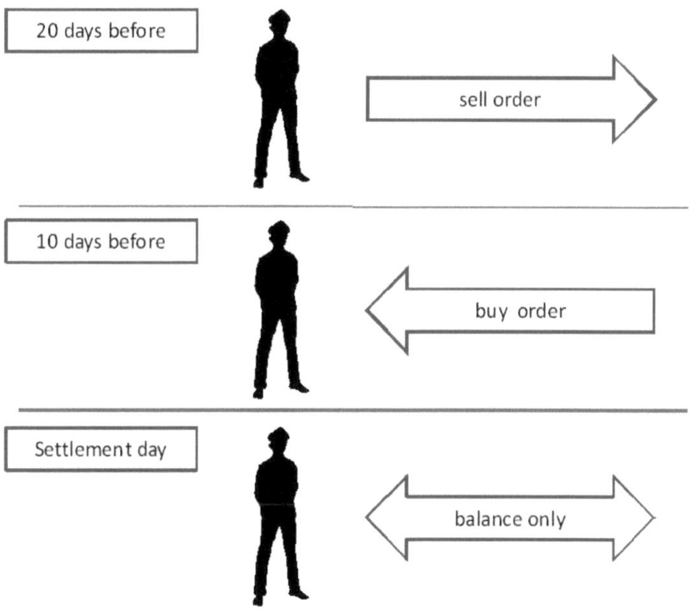


**Fig. 3.5** Netting

[4] For this reason, the sell order can be placed having no actual products at that moment, or without any buy order placed. This is called 'selling short.'

Example of netting

Table 3.3 shows the example where netting results in a positive value. After selling 1,000 units at 103 yen each, the trader in this example bought back 300 units at 97 yen each; 700 units at 105 yen each. In this example, he will receive a positive value worth 400 yen from the exchange as a balance.

Table 3.4 shows the example of selling 600 units at 103 each and 400 units at 100 yen each; buying 300 units at 97 yen each and 700 units at 105 yen each, which resulted in a negative value worth 800 yen as total.

Where buying and selling does not balance at the contract month

When positions are not zero at the contract month, the ownership right actually moves. The actual product is received if there is a buying position. If there is a selling position, the actual product that was obtained from the spot market should be received. If the actual product corresponding to the futures product is one that does not exist, just like stock-index futures products handled by U-Mart, netting has taken place assuming that selling positions (buying positions) finally left are balanced by the close of trading on the spot price of the final day.

**Table 3.3** Example of netting (the case of positive value)

| class | price (JPY) | volume (unit) | change in account (JPY) |
|---|---|---|---|
| sell | 103 | 1,000 | +103,000 |
| buy | 97 | 300 | −29,100 |
| buy | 105 | 700 | −73,500 |
| total | | | +400 |

**Table 3.4** Example of netting (the case of negative value)

| class | price (JPY) | volume (unit) | change in account (JPY) |
|---|---|---|---|
| sell | 103 | 600 | +61,800 |
| buy | 97 | 300 | −29,100 |
| Sell | 100 | 400 | +40,000 |
| buy | 105 | 700 | −73,500 |
| total | | | −800 |

Margin system

Upon starting futures trading, all the cash required for trading at the present stage does not have to be available. In the futures market, coming before trading, the exchange demands margin money of 2 percent to 5 percent of trading turnover for market participants. Margin money proves the participant's ability to pay, when a transaction results in a negative value at the due date.

As a result of Mark-to-Market, the exchange daily increases or decreases the balances of accounts of participants' margin money. When margin money falls below the minimum limit price, the exchange demands additional margin money (this is called 'maintenance margin'). At the due date, in the case of positive value the trading result is added to margin money or in the case of negative value it is deducted. In this way the balance of the participant's margin money is maintained and the fulfillment of transactions are guaranteed with such a system.

The margin system is beneficial, not only for the safe trading performance, but also for market participants themselves. This is known as the 'leverage effect.' The requirement of margin money, which is from 2 percent to 5 percent of trading turnover, means that it is possible to trade using the money resources that is 20 to 50 times more than what is available at first. This indicates that a more effective money management method is used than borrowing the same amount from a money resource to trade on an ordinary stock market. In addition, this is also a factor for attracting many traders.

### *3.2.5 How Orders and Contracts are Taken Place*

Orders

Customers place orders specifying the following items:

- Brand name
- Sell or buy
- Order volume
- Price idea

There are two ways to specify the price idea:

- Market order: An order to require the trade at the price established on the market, regardless of how much the price is formed by the market.
- Limit order: An order to require the trade at a price specified by a trader, setting as a limit value (lower limit when selling, upper limit when buying).

The buy order of the limit price $p$ is an order that buys when the price is below $p$, and does not buy if this is not the case. The sell order of the limit price $p$ is an order that sells when the price is over $p$, and does not sell if this is not the case. In other words, the limit order can be received only if the trade results in the gain of additional profits in relation to the specified price.

Contracts

In the actual market like the Tokyo Stock Exchange, order processing is different depending on when opening the market and when the market is already opened.

The following three kinds of order processing have been adopted in Japan's stock exchanges.

- *Itayose* trading session: This is usually conducted upon opening of the market. This processing collects the orders (boards) that have already been received before the opening of the market, and establishes the transactions at the price that agrees with the trade turnover.
- *Itaawase* trading session: This is similar to *Itayose*; this processing establishes the transactions in the price when the trade turnover reaches its maximum.
- Continuous auction session: When the market is already opened, this processing establishes the transactions by identifying the order that has already been placed, and each time an order is received as needed.

The actual Itayose trading session algorithm is as follows.

Itayose algorithm

Where $b_i = (p_{bi}, q_{bi})$ is a sell order, $s_j = (p_{sj}, q_{sj})$ is a buy order, $i$ and $j$ expresses the number of orders, $p_*$ is an order price, $q_*$ is an order volume, the market order price for a buy order is 0 as a matter of convenience, the market order price for a sell order is the same price with the maximum order price, the following formula expresses demand $B(p)$ and supply $S(p)$ when the price is $p$.

$$B(p) = \sum_{i, p_{bi} \geq p} q_{bi} = \sum q_{bi} - \sum_{i, p_{bi} < p} q_{bi}$$

$$S(p) = \sum_{j, p_{sj} \leq p} q_{sj}$$

There is no guarantee that $p*$ that becomes $B(p*) = S(p*)$ exists uniquely since the orders are discrete. $p$ that becomes $B(p) = S(p)$ can exist in the interval, or $p$ that becomes $B(p) = S(p)$ does not exist. When $p$ that becomes $B(p) = S(p)$ does not exist, the price is determined between minimum $p*$ that becomes $B(p*) \geq S(p*)$ and maximum $p*$ that becomes $B(p*) \leq S(p*)$. In U-Mart, the contract price is defined as $\frac{p^* * p_*}{2}$.[5]

[5] Confirm that this definition includes the case when p* is unique.

Example shown by a graph

Using the specific numerical example, let us create the actual board to draw the demand curve and the supply curve.[6] As an example, the orders shown in Table 3.5 are placed.

At first, collect all the orders of the members to list them in a table format, separating them into buying and selling. The orders are listed in the order from low price, however, since the limit sell order is an order that can sell in any price, the limit sell orders comes first regarding them as a 0-yen orders. Additionally, the limit buy orders are orders that can buy in any price, so the limit buy order comes last of buy orders having the highest price (Table 3.6).

Next, the order volume at each limit price and the cumulative order volume of each price are calculated. The sell orders are orders that sell if the price is higher than a certain value, so the cumulative order volume is calculated from the lower price. On the other hand, since the buy orders are an orders that buys only if the price is lower than a certain value, the cumulative order volume is calculated from the higher price. In other words, both buying and selling orders, the cumulative order volume is calculated from the side which the limit orders is listed (Table 3.7).

Finally, a table is created, which lists the cumulative order volume of buying and selling according to each price. In the price portion on any one of whether buying

**Table 3.5** Order List

| Trader | sell / buy | Market / Limit | Price | Order volume |
|---|---|---|---|---|
| 1 | sell | Limit | 2,800 | 10 |
| 2 | buy | Limit | 2,800 | 20 |
| 3 | buy | Limit | 3,100 | 20 |
| 4 | sell | Limit | 2,550 | 15 |
| 5 | buy | Limit | 3,100 | 25 |
| 6 | sell | Limit | 2,300 | 20 |
| 7 | buy | Market | - | 5 |
| 8 | sell | Limit | 3,200 | 20 |
| 9 | sell | Market | - | 10 |
| 10 | sell | Limit | 3,200 | 30 |
| 11 | sell | Limit | 2,550 | 15 |
| 12 | buy | Limit | 3,100 | 20 |
| 13 | buy | Limit | 3,400 | 20 |
| 14 | buy | Limit | 3,100 | 45 |
| 15 | sell | Limit | 2,800 | 20 |

[6] This numerical example is taken from the exercise assigned to the participants at the annual U-Mart summer school (created by Kita, Kyoto University).

**Table 3.6** Creating the tables according to buying and selling

| Sell orders | | | | Buy orders | | | |
|---|---|---|---|---|---|---|---|
| Trader | Market / Limit | Price | Order volume | Trader | Market / Limit | Price | Order volume |
| 10 | Limit | 3,200 | 30 | 7 | Market | | 5 |
| 8 | Limit | 3,200 | 20 | 13 | Limit | 3,400 | 20 |
| 15 | Limit | 2,800 | 20 | 14 | Limit | 3,100 | 45 |
| 1 | Limit | 2,800 | 10 | 12 | Limit | 3,100 | 20 |
| 11 | Limit | 2,550 | 15 | 5 | Limit | 3,100 | 25 |
| 4 | Limit | 2,550 | 15 | 3 | Limit | 3,100 | 20 |
| 6 | Limit | 2,300 | 20 | 2 | Limit | 2,800 | 20 |
| 9 | Market | | 10 | | | | |

**Table 3.7** Cumulative order volume

| Sell orders | | | Buy orders | | |
|---|---|---|---|---|---|
| Trader | Price | Cumulative order volume | Trader | Price | Cumulative order volume |
| 8,10 | 3,200 | 140 | 7 | 3,400~ | 5 |
| 1,15 | 2,800 | 90 | 13 | 3,400 | 25 |
| 4,11 | 2,550 | 60 | 3,5,12,14 | 3,100 | 135 |
| 6 | 2,300 | 30 | 2 | 2,800 | 155 |
| 9 | ~2,300 | 10 | | | |

or selling, the low cumulative production volume is entered if it is a sell order, and the high cumulative production volume is entered if it is a buy order (Table 3.8).

Comparing the difference between buy and sell order volumes in the list of cumulative production volume according to the price, the point showing the smallest balance between both volumes is the price that is established in the market. For the

**Table 3.8** List of cumulative production volumes according to prices

| Sell orders | Price | Buy orders |
|---|---|---|
| 140 | 3,400~ | 5 |
| 140 | 3,400 | 25 |
| 90 | 3,200 | 25 |
| 90 | 3,100 | 135 |
| 90 | 2,800 | 155 |
| 60 | 2,550 | 155 |
| 30 | 2,300 | 155 |
| 10 | ~2,300 | 155 |

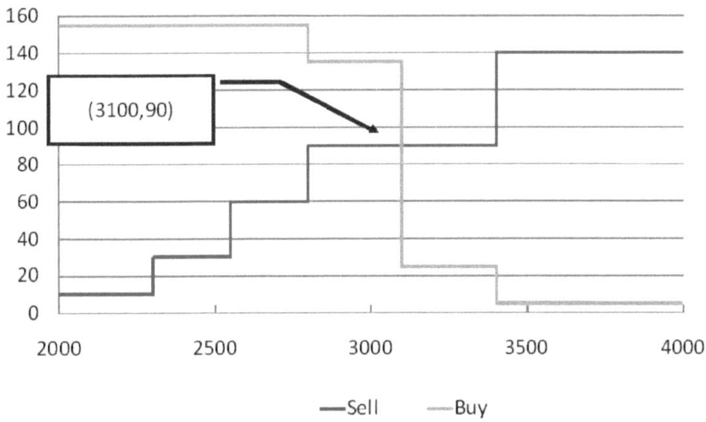


**Fig. 3.6** Determination of price and volume

buy and sell volumes at that time, the established price are adopted if both volumes, sell and buy, correspond to each other. If the volumes are different, the smaller price is adopted. In this numerical example, the trading volume becomes 90.

At this time, on the seller's side, only those traders who bid until the cumulative orders become 90 from low price (1, 4, 6, 9, 11, and 15) can buy only their own order volumes. On the buyer's side, only those traders who bid until the cumulative orders become 25 (7, 13) can sell their own order volumes. There are 115 units of orders with 3,100 yen offered as a bid, so only the 60 units are contracted out of the orders placed by traders in 3,100 yen (3, 5, 12, and 14). No transaction is made for the sell orders higher than 3,100 yen and the buy orders lower then 3,100 yen. Which and whose order is contracted depends on the market rules, such as time priority (first-come-first-serve), and proportional allotment according to the order volume. In this numerical example, "3,100" is the price and "90" is the volume, which have been determined respectively.

Fig. 3.6 shows what it would be like if the same process is graphically shown. For the convenience of explanation, the horizontal axis indicates the price; however, this figure shows the demand curve (buy order) and the supply curve (sell order) that are the same ones with what an economics textbook would contain.

## 3.3 Stock Index Futures Trading in Japan

The stock price index, the weighted average of several stocks, is relatively a more stable than the volatile price individual stocks. For this reason, stock index futures trading are very popular aiming for the risk hedge of stock investment. The stock price index can be broadly categorized under the following two types: simple average index and capitalization weighted index. The simple average index takes into consideration the market's rate levels and its transitions, whereas the capitalization weighted index takes into consideration the transition of the entire asset value. In the world stock indexes, the simple average index or all-brand index is less popular than the capitalization weighted index that is a brand-extraction based index.

Stock index futures trading targets the abstract numeric value, that is a stock index. Therefore, it never has the products actually delivered. Hence, net trading is taken place as the settlement of stock index futures trading, not only in the settlement by reselling and repurchasing but also in the final settlement by the due date. According to the Osaka Securities Exchange [39], the following points can be cited as the functions of stock index futures trading combined with ordinary futures trading functions:

1. Stock index futures trading offers corporate traders holding many stock brands a place to hedge the price volatility risks of the entire stock market effectively, with the changes in economic situation.
2. Stock index futures trading serve to stabilize and expand the trading market through the arbitrage transaction between futures and spot products.
3. The way of delivery risk aversion is opened, which leads to stabilizing and expanding the issue market.
4. The future expected price is independently formed with the opening of the futures market, so that the price formation in the spot futures market becomes more accurate. With that, the quality of price information is improved.
5. New investing methods are provided.

From the following section, specific stock indexes are introduced.

### 3.3.1 Nikkei Index (Nikkei 225)

This index was introduced by the Osaka Securities Exchange beginning in September, 1988. Nikkei 225 is the simple average of 225 stock brands; however, it has been revised in order that factors other than market fluctuations can be prevented from affecting on Nikkei 225. The causes of stock price volatility other than market fluctuations include stock splits; ex-rights due to capital increase, mergers, and reverse stock splits.

How to calculate Nikkei 225

$$\text{Nikkei 225} = (\text{Sum stock price of 225 stock brands})/\text{the divisor}$$

The divisor is the number of stock brands basically, but it is revised appropriately.

Example of revising the divisor

Let us consider the following example of stock brands and prices.

- Brand A: 1,000 yen
- Brand B: 2,000 yen
- Brand C: 3,000 yen

In this case, the average stock price of these three brands is 2,000 yen calculated by the following: $(1,000+2,000+3,000)/3=2,000$. Here, if the company C conducts the stock split of 1:1.2, the stock price becomes 2,500 yen ($3,000/1.2=2,500$). If the divisor remains the same value, the average stock price of these three brands is 1,833 yen, but this price fall is due to a stock split, not a market fluctuation. In order to remove the influence of stock split, the devisor of denominator is revised as follows.

$$\begin{aligned}&\text{New devisor}\\&\quad=\{\text{Present devisor}\times(\text{Sum stock price of the three brands in the previous day}\\&\qquad-\text{The right price})\}/\text{Sum stock price of the previous day}\end{aligned}$$

In this case, the right price is 500 yen (3,000 yen – 2,500 yen), so the new devisor is to be 2.75 calculated by following: $3\times(6,000-500)/6,000=2.75$. Dividing the stock price by the new devisor, it would be the following calculation: $(1,000+2,000+2,500)/2.75=2,000$. Now it has been found that the devisor is revised properly.

### *3.3.2 Nikkei Stock Index 300 (Nikkei 300)*

Nikkei 300 is the capitalization weighted index created for the 300 major stock brands that are listed on the first section of the Tokyo Stock Exchange. Nippon Keizai Shimbun developed this index, and the Osaka Securities Exchange has started using this index beginning in February, 1994. The Nikkei 300 consists of the stock brands having significant size of enterprise, taking into consideration liquidity and enterprise performance. For that reason, the structure of Nikkei 300 is well-balanced in the industrial sectors, being rich in the market and industry representation.

How to calculate Nikkei 300

To calculate Nikkei 300, the stock price is multiplied by the number of issued stocks according to each stock brand regarding its components. Then, the ‘total market value’ that aggregates all the components is divided by the total market value at the base point of time (1 October, 1982), and expressed in percentage.

$$\text{Nikkei 300} = (\text{the total market value at calculation}) / \text{the standard total market value} \times 100$$

However, whenever certain factors occur to cause a reshuffle of the adopted stock brands such as ex-rights of paid-in capital increase, public offering and third-party allocation, stock conversion of convertible bonds and preferred stocks, and mergers, the standard total market value is revised as follows.

$$\begin{aligned}&\text{'New' standard total market value}\\&\quad = \text{Old standard total market value} \times (\text{the total market value before revision}\\&\qquad \pm \text{the revised total market value}) / \text{the total market value before revision}\end{aligned}$$

## 3.3.3 Tokyo Stock Exchange Stock Price Index (TOPIX)

TOPIX is a market capitalization index consisting of all domestic companies of the exchange's First Section, which has been used since September, 1988. Considering the total market value at the point of January 4 in 1968, as the base point of time, TOPIX is an index created for the total market value after this base point of time.

How to calculate TOPIX

$$\text{TOPIX} = \text{the total market value at calculation} / \text{Standard total market value} \times 100$$

TOPIX considers all stock brands listed in the First Section when calculating the target weight of each number of listed stocks, so TOPIX reflects to some degree all the number of listing stocks. TOPIX is not vulnerable to the fluctuation by a small number of stock brands, but it is very sensitive to reflect the trends of large capital stocks that have many stockholders.

## 3.3.4 J30

J30 is a stock price index created by Mainichi Shimbun, and is the simple average of stock prices of Japan's 30 leading companies at the time (NTT and TEPCO were reevaluated by 50 yen per value). The revision of devisor is similar to Nikkei 225, so the detailed explanation is abbreviated here. J30 data can be obtained from the data of December 29 in 1989, which is the date when the Nikkei average posted an all-time high price.

The 30 companies at the time of creating the J30 index (November 1998) are as follows.

OBAYASHI CORPORATION, ASAHI BREWRIES, LTD., Shin-Etsu Chemical Co., LTD., Kao Corporation, SANKYO COMPANY, LIMITED, Takeda Pharmaceutical Company Limited, Fuji Photo Film Co., LTD., BRIDGESTONE CORPORATION, KOMATSU LTD., FUJITSU LIMITED, Matsushita Electric Industrial Co., Ltd., SONY CORPORATION, TDK Corporation, KYOSERA Corporation, Mitsubishi Heavy Industries, LTD., TOYOTA MOTOR CORPORATION, HONDA MOTOR CO., LTD., CANON INC., RICOH COMPANY, LTD., Dai Nippon Printing Co., Ltd., Mitsubishi Corporation, Ito-Yokado Co., LTD., The Bank of Tokyo-Mitsubishi UFJ, Ltd., Sumitomo Mitsui Banking Corporation, Nomura Securities CO., LTD., Mitsui Fudosan Co., Ltd. YAMATO TRANSPORT CO., LTD., Nippon Telegraph and Telephone Corporation, Tokyo Electric Power Company, Incorporated., SECOM Co., Ltd.

The 30 companies after April $23^{rd}$ 2000 are as follows.

OBAYASHI CORPORATION, ASAHI BREWRIES, LTD., Shin-Etsu Chemical Co., LTD., Kao Corporation, SANKYO COMPANY, LIMITED, Takeda Pharmaceutical Company Limited, Fuji Photo Film Co., LTD., BRIDGESTONE CORPORATION, RICOH COMPANY, LTD., Hitachi, Ltd., FUJITSU LIMITED, Matsushita Electric Industrial Co., Ltd., SONY CORPORATION, TDK Corporation, FANUC LTD., KYOSERA Corporation, CANON INC., TOYOTA MOTORE CORPORATION, HONDA MOTOR CO., LTD., Dai Nippon Printing Co., Ltd., Mitsubishi Corporation, Ito-Yokado Co., LTD., The Bank of Tokyo-Mitsubishi UFJ, Ltd., Sumitomo Mitsui Banking Corporation, ORIX Corporation, Nomura Securities CO., LTD., YAMATO TRANSPORT CO., LTD., NTT, Tokyo Electric Power Company, Incorporated, SECOM Co., Ltd.

## 3.4 Investing Basics

There is only one way to make a profit as a trader participating in the futures market. No profit can be made unless there is a spread between buying and selling, there is no other way than to "buy low and sell high." The problem is how we can know 'the best time to sell at a high price' and 'the best time to buy at a low price.' This problem, in essence, means how to predict the future price.

Price forecasting can broadly be categorized into the following two methods: fundamental analysis and technical analysis. Fundamental analysis is a method that evaluates the adequate price level theoretically based on fundamentals (economic fundamental conditions) information such as interest-rate level, industrial trend, or economic trend. Technical analysis is a method that predicts the future price from the price transition patterns. This section introduces the basic concept of these two price forecasting methods.[7]

[7] This section describes just a simple concept. Refer to respective specialized books for details.

### *3.4.1 Fundamental Analysis*

Effective Market Hypothesis

This investing style is based on fundamental analysis to obtain a return rate of investment that exceeds the market average by the process of market price correction, buying (selling) if the market price is undervalued (overvalued) compared to fundamentals. It is not unusual that such stock prices show a significant divergence from the proper level, in view of fundamentals. However, the basic assumption of fundamental analysis is confidence in the market that "no matter how such non-fundamental factors like market participants' psychological factors influence on the market on a short-term basis, in a medium- and long-term perspective, the price converges with the proper level in view of fundamentals."

Effective Market Hypothesis is what supports this basic concept above. The specific definition of this hypothesis is described as follows.

> Where the bond price moves reflecting all sorts of information perfectly, it is impossible for a particular trader to expect to receive a higher profit consistently, more than the profit of all the investors participating in the market receive [7].

Plainly speaking, the effective market hypothesis is the concept that "the market becomes effective as long as people act reasonably seeking profits," and "it is impossible to gain a profit significantly exceeding the average market performance as long as the market is effective."[8] According to Shreifer [16], the effective market hypothesis is explained with the following three phases leveling the hypothesis gradually.

1. Traders evaluate securities reasonably because they are rational.
2. Even if there are some irrational traders, they will be balanced without affecting the trading price if their transactions are made randomly.
3. Although traders' irrationality has the same tendency, the irrational influence on the price is removed by the power of people who conduct rational arbitrage transactions in the market.

Namely, even if the security prices deviate from the proper price according to the conduct of irrational traders (they are called 'noise traders' in terms of judging buying and selling based on inappropriate information), it is considered that, in the long term, the price comes back to the proper price level by means of the arbitrage transactions by rational traders who judge based on accurate information.

The effective market hypothesis is divided into the following three phases, weak, semi-strong, and strong, in accord with the strength of efficiency for claimed information.

[8] The expression "effective" indicates that there is no any further opportunity to pursue profits as a result of proper resource allocation.

1. Weak form efficiency: Based on the past price and return knowledge, it is impossible for traders to make a profit that exceeds the average market performance.[9]
2. Semi-strong form efficiency: Based on open information, it is impossible for traders to make a profit that exceeds the average market performance.
3. Strong form efficiency: Based on inside information, it is impossible for traders to make a profit that exceeds the average market performance.

General traders who conduct fundamental analysis evaluate the effective market hypothesis at the level of weak and semi-strong forms; however, it is believed that they do not evaluate the hypothesis in the level of strong form. Additionally, they admit that, in the short term, that price do deviate from the fundamental price. It is natural because the price divergence from the fundamental price in the short term generates such profit opportunities.

From the standpoint of an effective market hypothesis that the security price is determined perfectly and effectively, daily price fluctuation is due to the price adjustment based on publicly disclosed information, or the fluctuation is no more than random shaking as an error. This is referred to as "Random Walk Hypothesis."

Stock investment measure

There are many types of stock investment measure; however, the most basic measures are the following three:

*Dividend Yield*

This is given by the following calculation: (expected dividends per a stock) / (stock price). Viewing a stock as a bond yields dividends, this is what is used to calculate a dividend yield. Where the dividend yield is more significant than the market interest rate (to be precise, a price added by some risks like company's bankruptcy and stock splitting to the market interest rate), it can be considered as a reason for purchase.

*PBR (Price Book-value Ratio)*

This is given by the following calculation: (stock price) / (net assets). This expresses whether it is possible to gain higher assets than the stock purchase value, if a company balances its accounts. It expresses a sell order if this value is greater than '1' which means the market overestimates the corporate value, whereas it expresses a buy order if this value is smaller than '1' which means the market underestimates the corporate value. PBR evaluates the asset with against book value, while an index t evaluates the asset against the current price is called 'Q ratio.'

[9] This is a concept that denies technical analysis introduced in the next section.

*PER (Price Earnings Ratio)*

This ratio is given by the following calculation: (stock price) / (profit per one stock). Considering the PER of the market average as the heating degree of the stock market, the company's PER and the PER of market average (varies depending on country or age) are compared and then the stock is judged whether it is undervalued or not.

### 3.4.2 Technical Analysis

Theoretical Environment over Technical Analysis

The name "technical analysis" indicates a general price forecasting method which predicts the price by extracting some kind of patterns from price transitions. This method has an old history (older history than the establishment of modern economics). This method is used by professional traders actually; however, it has been previously indicated that this method's theoretical foundation is weak compared to fundamental analysis.

Recently, however, the circumstances have been changed. Many phenomena have been discovered that the effective market hypothesis cannot explain, called "Anomaly," in the market price fluctuation [24]. Additionally, the field of "Behavioral Finance" that examines the psychological influence for decision making of market participants has become popular, and it has shown that a significant bias can be observed in humans' decision making.[10]

Furthermore, through research on the distribution of the price fluctuation band in foreign exchange rates, the following point has been found: although correlation can be observed between the price fluctuation band of previous and present time and the price fluctuation band of present time and future time, correlation with the further price band (the price fluctuation band that is determined in the future time and afterwards) shows the value of '0'. This point itself seems to indicate the random walk hypothesis. However, in volatility (time series correlation of price fluctuation absolute value), it is believed that there is a strong correlation from 0.2 to 0.3 which continues over long periods of time [19]. This indicates that once the market enters in a condition of violent price fluctuations, the condition continues for a while. This is a noteworthy result from the viewpoint of technical analysis, in it that tries to make a prediction from price transition information.

[10] When Daniel Kahneman was awarded the Nobel Prize in economics in 2002, one of the reasons for his prize was "a contribution to building the fundamental theory of behavioral finance."

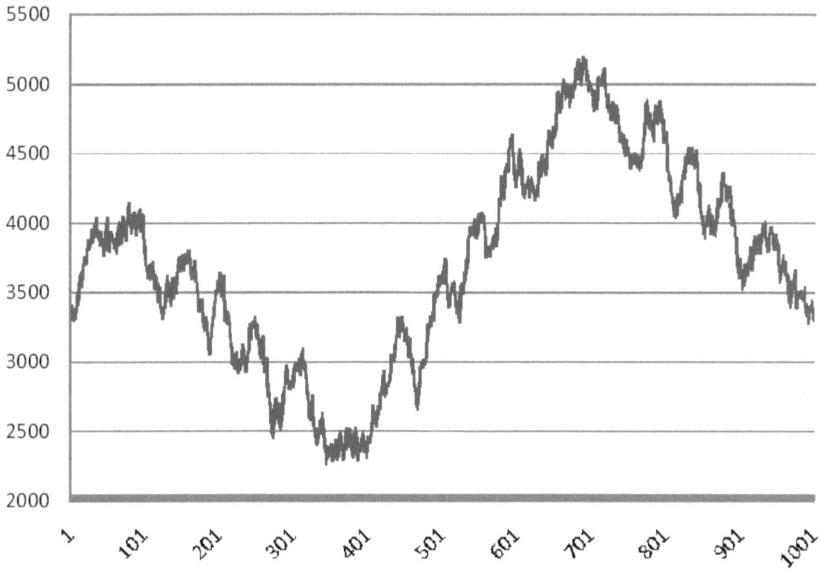


**Fig. 3.7** Virtual stock price line chart

Peaks and Valleys of Stock Price

Fig. 3.7 shows the virtual time series of stock price created artificially for this explanation. In this line chart, there is one peak of high prices before and after 50 points; the price goes down repeating small up and downs, and then the price stays at the bottom around 350 points. After that, the stock price started turning over and achieves the highest value greater than the first peak around a 700 points, and then the price suffers a downturn again.

If it is possible to discern two peaks and one significant valley, you can make a profit by buying at the peaks and selling at the valley. Moreover, if you are able to observe smaller up and downs between big peak and valleys, it must be possible to make more profits from those up and downs.

The stock price is fluctuating up and down minutely. From the fluctuation, it is necessary to distinguish big changes that form peaks and valleys from small daily changes. The moving-average method is one of the ways to draw such big trends only, ignoring those small fluctuations.

How to Calculate Moving Average

Moving Average is an index which consecutively calculates the average value for a certain period. Where a price at the time $t$ is $P(t)$, the moving average price of period $n$ at the time $t$ is $MAt(n)$, the definition of $MAt(n)$ is given by the following calculation.

$$MA_t(n) = \frac{1}{n}\sum_{i=0}^{n-1} P(t-1)$$

Where the moving average is MAt(10) (the moving average for 10 periods), the index of MAt(10) is the average index of P(t), P(t−1), P(t−2),..., and P(t−9). Thereafter, ones that can take the average, including the term that is to be counted first, are plotted. Taking the moving average balances of the slight fluctuation of each term, it allows finding out broad tendencies of the changes in prices. When the term is too long to take the average, the peaks and valleys might be also averaged; you need to adjust the length of the moving average according to the interval which you want to observe.

From Fig. 3.7, the following things are plotted in Fig. 3.8 (a): the prices of 300 terms right before the first valley (Price: solid line), the 10-time moving average (MA10: dotted line), the 30-time moving average (MA30: bold dotted-and-dashed line). It shows that when the average is taken over a long term, slight fluctuations are balanced and it makes the smooth line.

Fig. 3.8 (b) shows the 30-time moving average (MA30: dotted line) and the 100-time moving average (MA100: bold solid line), combined with what is shown in

**Fig. 3.8** Moving Average

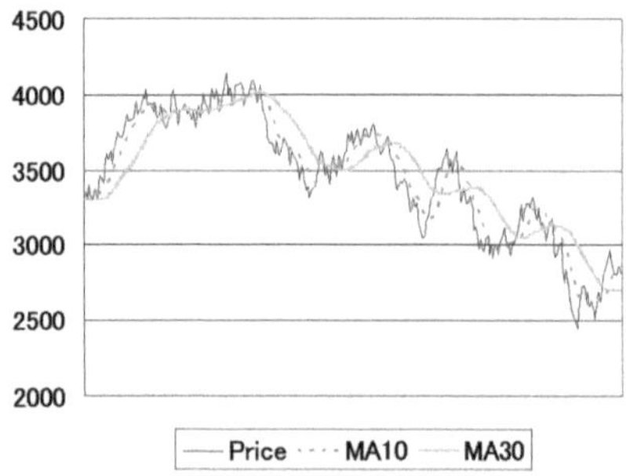


(a) The moving average of the first 300 terms

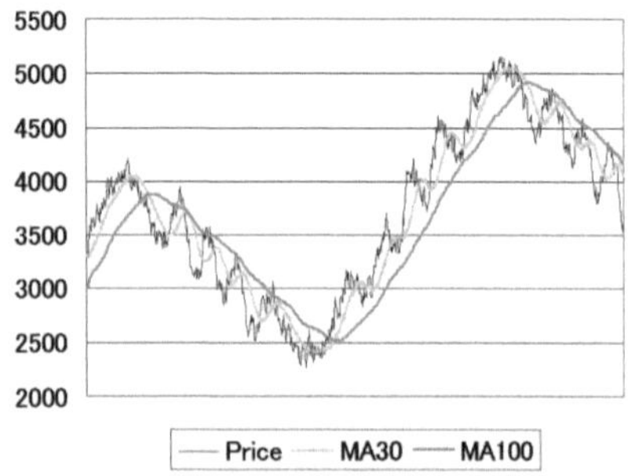


(b) The moving average of the entire terms

Fig. 3.7. It shows that MA30 goes up and down tracing small peaks, whereas MA100 shows the most typical tendency of price transition.

### Golden Cross and Dead Cross

If the moving average line removes slight fluctuations, that means, the moving average line can be the line that indicates the transition of broad equilibrium positions of sellers and buyers at that term. Therefore, the present market psychology can be grasped by comparing two moving average lines having different terms (the one having long term is called 'long-term moving average curve and the one having short term is called 'short-term moving average curve').

Where the short-term moving average curve is plotted below the long-term moving average curve, it can be said that the present price transition is below the long-term equilibrium position, and the market is occupied by a bearish trend (the recognition of downward trend in prices). In contrast, the short-term moving average curve is plotted above the long-term moving average curve; it can be considered that the market is in a bullish trend (the recognition of upward trend in prices).

At the point in time, where the short-term moving average curve intersects with the long-term moving average curve, is the point in time where the market makes a shift from bearish trend to bullish trend (or bullish trend to bearish trend), and this point in time is an important factor for judging market conditions.

When the short-term moving average curve intersects with the long-term moving average curve from below, this is called the golden cross. Where the golden cross is observed, it can be expected that the price moves upwards from now because the market is powerful in short term. On the contrary, when the short-term moving average curve intersects with the long-term moving average curve from above, this is called the dead cross. Where the dead cross is observed, it can be expected that the price falls off from then (Fig. 3.9 (a)).

Fig. 3.9 (b) shows the marked portions where the golden cross and dead cross are observed from the price transition shown in Fig. 3.8 (b). It shows that the golden cross and dead cross are occurring at the turning-point of a big price trend.

Since the moving average is taken, the point to notice is that the golden cross and dead cross delay in occurring when compared to the actual turning-point of price trend. With this reason, there is a possibility to miss an opportunity to buy and sell when the price fluctuates wildly.

### Market Following and Contrary

Suppose, a price moves upwards in a market and moves much further. Profits can be gained by buying at this point and selling when the price starts falling off. This method, buying when the price moves upwards and selling when the price falls off, is called the "Market following" investment style (market follower) because the method is in accordance with price movements.

**Fig. 3.9** Golden cross and Dead cross

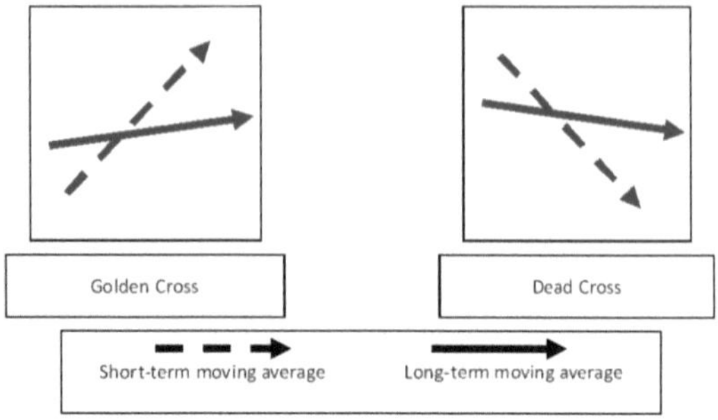


(a) Concept

(b) Example on the price transition

On the other hand, profits can be gained by selling at the point where the price rose adequately and buying at the point where the price fell off substantially This method, selling when the price moves upwards and buying when the price falls off, is called the "Contrary" investment style (contrarian) (Fig. 3.10).

Each style has its own drawbacks and advantages. Since the market followers buy when the price moves upwards (when the buy orders concentrate) and sell when the price falls off (when the sell orders concentrate), so they face in the same judging direction with other market participants. The market followers belong to the majority in the market; it is easy to confirm their own judgments. Additionally, the market following investment style is easy to predict the price because the market followers just need to judge the time point when the price trend is formed. However, in this investment style, the orders are placed at the time point when the orders are concentrated, so there is a possibility that traders cannot buy and sell with the limit price they speculate, due to a significant price movement than what is expected. It is especially, it is dangerous to place a market order with the market following investment style because it might lead to buying at an extraordinary high price (or selling at an extraordinary low price).

In contrast, the contrary investment style is the opposite method to the market following investment style, so that it can be considered that the contrarians belong to

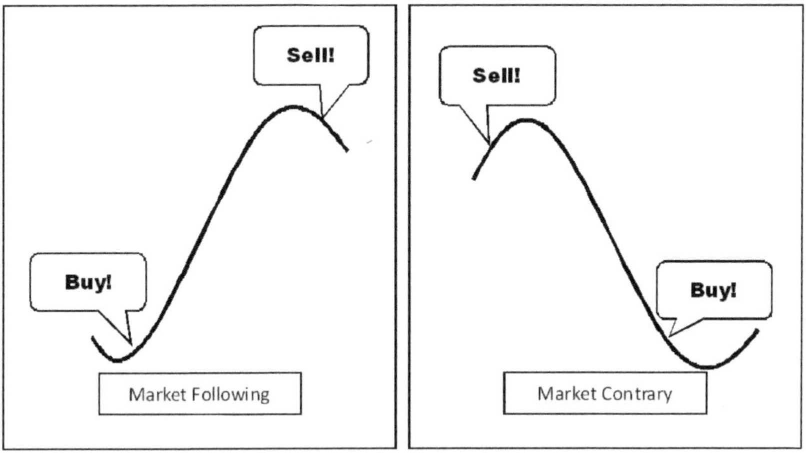


**Fig. 3.10** Market following and Contrary

the minority in the market. It is hard to gain profits with the contrary investment style because this method has a possibility to incur a loss if the price continues moving upwards after selling when the price started rising. However, the opposite orders are concentrated so it is easy for the contrarians to trade within their speculated price with the limit orders. Furthermore, market events such as skyrocketing prices or plunges in prices draw the price in a direction to contrarians' advantage, which allows reducing the risk of placing the market orders.

Realized Profit and Loss Cut

An unrealized profit is made with Mark-to-Market when the market price continues moving upwards (falling off) with long (short) positions held, however, the profit is not confirmed yet. A closed trade should be conducted in order to confirm the unrealized profit as an actual profit. This transaction confirming the profit is called "realized profit."

On the other hand, the unrealized loss is made with Mark-to-Market when the market price continues falling off (moving upwards) with short (long) positions held. The transaction, confirming the loss with the closed trade in order to prevent the loss from increasing, is called "loss cut."

## 3.5 Artificial Market Study and U-Mart

### *3.5.1 What is an Artificial Market?*

An artificial market is a generic term for the study that conducts a simulation on the virtual market using computers.[11] The best achievement of econophysics and the artificial market study is that the model has been built, which model can explain the occurrence of price fluctuation distribution[12] presented as evidence to prove that an effective market hypothesis cannot be established.

U-Mart is also an artificial market; however, the model structure is different from other artificial market models. Thus, it shows U-Mart's originality. This section introduces the artificial market studies other than U-Mart.

Common Structure of Market Model

Basically, a market model progresses by collecting the micro-level orders $O = \{o^1, o^2, \cdots o^n\}$ that are placed by each agent. This is done in order to obtain the price $P$ that is a macro variable and the result $X = \{x^1, x^2, \cdots x^n\}$ from the resource allocation for each agent. In the market model, the market matches the micro-level orders to produce macro-level price, at the same time, the market serves as a 'black box' that gives feedback from the resource allocation at micro-level of each agent (Fig. 3.11). This series of flow, from the aggregation of orders to price and resource allocation decisions, is viewed as one unit time.

Regarding the price P and resource allocation results outputted by the market, there are some variations according to kind and volume of products to be handled; however, no essential differences exist in each market model.

The significant difference between each market model is that the orders can be viewed as input from the market, or they can be viewed as output from each agent. Since the orders become different depending on the agent's decision-making model, it is natural that the calculation of price and resource allocation differs according to the orders. With that, it can be considered that the market model consists of the following two parts: the 'interface part' that receives orders from agents and the 'computing engine part' that aggregates orders to calculate the price and conduct resource allocation.

---

[11] For the survey of existing model, refer to *Introduction to Artificial Market* written by Isamu Izumi and Kazuhiro Ueda, and see the report of Artificial Intelligence Study Group of Information Processing Society of Japan, Vol. 99, pp.9-17, 2000. There is another artificial market study other than the financial market, but it is beyond of this book's scope.

[12] In the effective market hypothesis, the size of individual price fluctuation is regarded as a normal distribution. The actual market often takes the index near to the average than the normal distribution; the index significantly away from the average (the index $3\sigma$ or $4\sigma$ away) is also generated with almost impossible frequency in the normal distribution hypothesis. It is called "High peak, fat tail" because of the above mentioned two qualities. Refer to [19] for details.

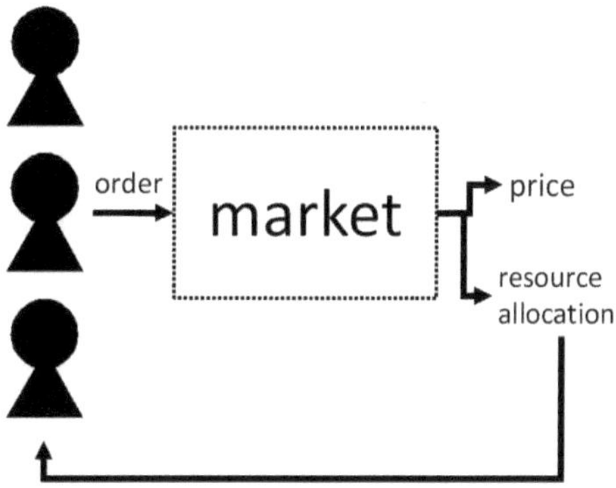


**Fig. 3.11** Basic structure of market model

The models in the artificial market study can broadly be categorized into two types, the bid type and the function-send type (actually three types, if adding the 'particle type' that is somewhat exceptional econophysics model), as shown in Table 3.9.

The bid type is a model in which each agent places an order specifying order classification (sell/buy), order price, and order volume. This type is a near model to decision-making in the actual market, and U-Mart is categorized in the bid type. There is the continuous auction session as a decision method for price and resource allocation, other than the *Itayose* trading session.

The function-send type is a model in which each agent sends the demand function to the exchange, and aggregates it to decide the price and volume. This is the most common type used in artificial market modeling, and the function-send type has become popular because of the boom of interest generated when The Santa Fe Institute adopted the function-send type for the ASM (Artificial Stock Market).

The particle type is a model that tries to prepare many agents (sort of agents) defined by only the combination of two indexes, the sales price idea and purchase price idea, in order to describe price movements as a chain reaction between the particles.

**Table 3.9** The model structures of artificial market

| | Interface | Computing engine |
|---|---|---|
| Bid price | Send order classification (buy/sell), order price, and order volume | Itayose trading session / Continuous auction session |
| Function-send type | Send the demand function | Partial equilibrium |
| Particle type (Econophysics model) | Spread | One-on-one matching |

### 3.5.2 Bid Type

*Itayose* trading session

Since the *Itayose* trading session is able to handle large orders at one time, nowadays, it is utilized in the transactions of morning and afternoon sessions (at start-up) and the opening auction (at transaction ended) in the Tokyo Stock Exchange. The *Itayose* trading session's algorithm has been already described, so this section does not give an explanation about the algorithm.

Characteristics of the *Itayose* trading session

Differing from the continuous auction session shown in the next section, the *Itayose* trading session has a significant fluctuation band when compared to the close price. This characteristic is attributable to the algorithm that collects all orders and handles them at one time.

Additionally, where there are large amounts of market orders and the orders with extremely high prices (or low prices), these transactions might be established with extremely high or low prices. This phenomenon is observed quite often in U-Mart; however, this phenomenon also occurs in the real market due to bidding without noticing whether the order price and the order volume are imputed reversely.

Continuous Auction Session

The continuous auction session is a method that handles transactions by matching the orders one after another according to the rules of 'time priority' and 'price priority.' Although this method is able to deal with price formation and transaction decision sequentially and promptly, this method is unsuitable for a time when large orders concentrate in the market. Because of this reason, the Tokyo Stock Exchange adopts this method in only during the hours between market start-up and the opening auction.

Quote Price and Ordering

In the continuous auction session, when the condition exists where the transaction is not established, the old orders are left remaining valid for quite a while. Once these valid orders are collected, it is referred to as a 'board' as is the case with the *Itayose* trading session. Out of those valid orders, the lowest sell order price is called the "ask quote price," and the highest buy order price is called "bid quote price."

Table 3.10 shows the order prices and order volumes that have remained without establishing the transaction, as a result of the *Itayose* trading session with the nu-

**Table 3.10** Board Example

| Buy/Sell | Order Price | Volume |
|---|---|---|
| Sell | 3,200 | 50 |
| Buy | 3,100 | 45 |
| Buy | 2,800 | 20 |

merical example of the section 3.5. At this time, the ask quote price became 3,200 and the bid quote price became 3,100.

An agent who places orders next refers to these quote prices to place orders. An agent who considers selling finds out that if the price is 3,100, there is no problem for 45 units to be sold right now. In this case, it is possible for the agent to achieve his goal by placing the market order or placing the limit order at 3,100.

When he wants to sell as soon as possible, but at a price higher than 3,100, he needs to place the order price lower than 3,200 and higher than 3,100, expecting the sell order higher than 3,100 will eventually be placed. On the contrary, when he does not feel pressed to sell, there is no problem with placing the sell order, having price higher than 3,200. In this case, all order is matched for the first time after handling all the sell orders having the price of 3,200.

Characteristics of Continuous Auction Session

Compared to the *Itayose* trading session, in the continuous auction session, prices have a moderate fluctuation band because the price moves between the ask quote price and bid quote price. In addition, since the continuous auction session corresponds to the real exchange system in its determination of price and transactions, further future research is expected in this method as an application of research on the daily price fluctuation estimate.

### *3.5.3 Function-Send Type*

The agent transmits the demand function to the market in each term, and the market calculates the demand function for each agent, in order to determine the equilibrium price and volume of the present period. This is how the function-send type works. To judge whether each agent purchased or sold, their holdings of the current term and previous term calculated from the equilibrium price and individual demand function are compared. Then it is determined in an ex-post way that the agent bought if the present term holding are larger, whereas the agent would have sold if the present term holdings are less.

Following from here is the explanation of the actual calculations in the simulation processes.

### Create Demand Function

Based on the information provided from the previous session, here, each agent creates the demand function $d^i(p)$ (Fig. 3.12).

$d^i(p)$ is the price response function that returns the value of stock amount $x^i$ held by the agent $i$ where is the market price is $p$. The information of orders, buying or selling, are not expressly presented to the agent, and the agent is unable to know whether he bought or sold, as well as his transaction volume, until the computing processing is finished in the exchange.

### Price Determination

The market collects demand functions of all the agents in order to create the demand function of the entire market. The supply function has a vertical line on the plain of price and volume, since the gross amount of stock issues is consistent. The intersection point of this vertical line with the demand function of entire market becomes the equilibrium price; the transaction is made with this price (Fig. 3.13).

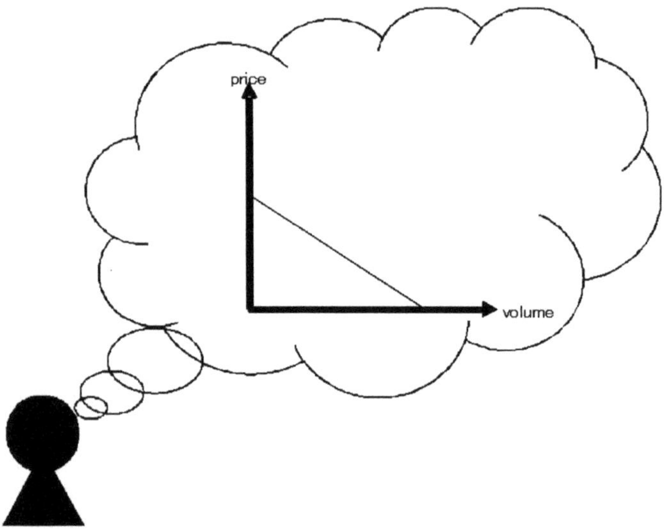


**Fig. 3.12** Creation of demand function

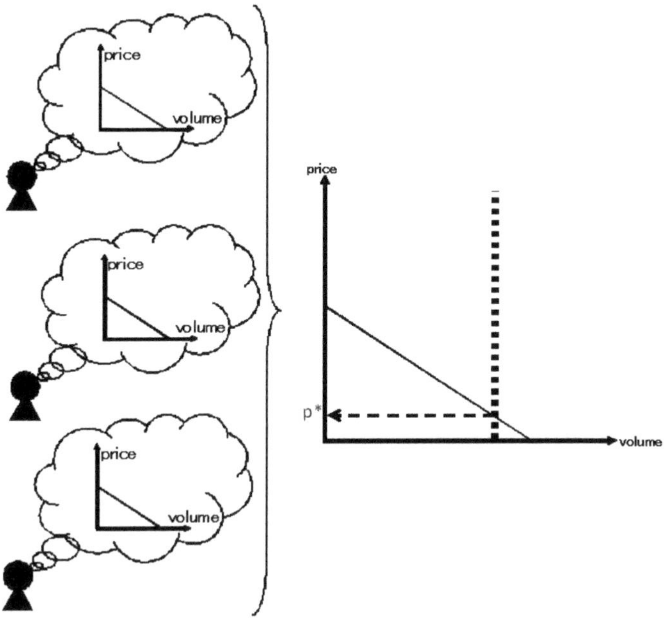


**Fig. 3.13** Price determination

Change in holdings of each agent

Assigning the equilibrium price $p^*$ to the demand function of each agent makes it possible to determine the holdings of each agent ($x^*$ in Fig. 3.14) at the end of the present session. The agent's trading volume is defined as the absolute value $|x^* - x'|$ of the difference in holdings at the onset of the session.

The agent's transaction is determined as buying where $x^* - x' > 0$ and as selling where$x^* - x' < 0$, in ex-post way.

About Agent's Demand Function

When it comes to the demand function that an agent transmits to the exchange, a model creator can create it arbitrarily. The individuality of each model can be observed in the following three things: the asset evaluation function of the agent (it might take the usual utility function form or another form), settings of price forecasting functions of next term, and the learning method of the forecasting function.

The following method was adopted by the ASM [9] of The Santa Fe Institute: a method that creates the demand function for risk asset prices taking into consideration the decision of orders as the portfolio selection problem between risk-free assets and risk assets. The CARA utility function $U(W) = -e^{-W}$ was adopted as the asset evaluation function, and the adaptive expectation was used for price forecast-

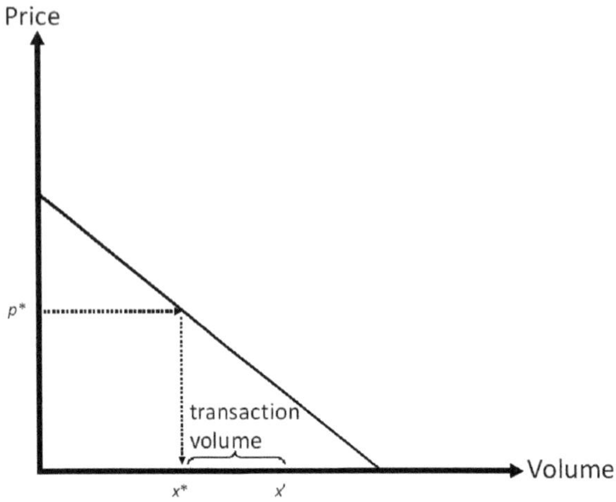


**Fig. 3.14** Price determination in ASM

ing. Where working out the solution to the expected utility maximization problem with this type of utility function, the solution becomes the simple linear function that is $x = \frac{a-bp}{c}$. This demand function is transmitted to the exchange.

Regarding the agent's evaluation function, it is possible to freely design it just like the one implementing the prospect theory by Kahneman & Tversky, or the one that responds to news as introduced by [5].

### *3.5.4 Particle Type*

There is a market model introduced by econophysicists, standing on a completely different viewpoint. From the viewpoint of physics, econophysics can be seen as one of the application fields of statistical physics using a wide variety of methods which have been developed in the field of statistical physics to analyze High Frequency Data. High Frequency Data indicates stock and bond price data in the field of economics; therefore, statistical physics analyzes the financial market mainly in view of a very short term.

The following two points are believed as a significant difference between the market model with an econophysical approach and another market model: 1), agents and the decision-making model have very simple structures, and 2) the number of agents is numerous. Another artificial market simulation has a complicated structure in the agent's decision making model, and enhances expressiveness with the complexity of interactions between environment (what calculates other agents' decisions) and the agent's decision making model. On the other hand, the econophysics market model adopts the extremely simple agent's decision making model, but improves on the model's expressiveness by the complexity of a chain reaction among a large number of agents instead.[13]

A model created by econophysists can be viewed that simplifies the continuous auction session to make the trading volume always become '1'. This is because the interests are concentrated on the portion that creates the model showing close distribution with statistical characteristics observed in High Frequency Data, so that the other portions should be made as simple as possible.

From Takayasu et al.[14], the following section introduces agent's decision making and pricing.

### Agent Modeling

On the time point $t$, the agent $i$ has the selling price idea *Si(t)* and the buying price idea *Bi(t)*. The spread between *Si(t)* and *Bi(t)* is defined as follows: $L = Si(t) - Bi(t)$. The value of L is common among respective agents, and is constant over time. Namely, the current condition of the agent $i$ is expressed by only the value of *Bi(t)*.

### Determination of Trading Price and State Variation of Agent

To establish the transaction between two agents of $i$ and $j$ at the time point $t$, one's buying price idea needs to exceed the other one's selling price idea. In other words, seeing agent $i$ as a seller and $j$ as a buyer, the following condition is what establishes the transaction:$B_i(t) > S_j(t) \Leftrightarrow B_i(t) - B_j(t) \geq L$.

When generalizing the condition in the entire market, the condition that establishes the transaction is as follows:

$$\max_i\{B_i(t)\} - \min_i\{B_i(t)\} \geq L \tag{3.1}$$

Where the transaction condition is not established, price ideas of all the agents are changed according to the rules of changes in price idea shown at the last.

Where the transaction condition is established, the highest buying price idea is set to the price $P(t)$ at the time point of $t$. Where the agent having the highest buying price idea buys one unit of stocks and the number of agents whose buying price idea meets the condition is $n$, the number of $n$ agents sells one unit per $n$, each.

After the transaction is over, buyers and sellers change the respective prices in$\Delta_i$. The price change band $\Delta_i$ is defined as follows:

---

[13] In a rough sense, where viewing the number of agents * the complexity of agent's decision making model as one indicator of model's expressiveness, no significant difference in its expressive power can be observed between both models.

[14] H. Takayasu et al., "Statical properties of deterministic threshold elements", *Physica*, A, pp.127-134, 1992.

$$\Delta_i = \begin{cases} -\delta, & \text{Buyers} \\ \delta/n, & \text{Sellers} \\ 0. & \text{Other than both} \end{cases} \quad (3.2)$$

For $\Delta_i$, using the parameter $a_i$ that expresses individual differences of each agent (easy to predict the price advance, or easy to predict the price drop) and the trend-following degree $c_i$, the following expression defines the price idea Bi(t+1) of agent $i$ at the time (t + 1).

$$B_i(t+1) = B_i(t) + \Delta_i(t) + a_i + c_i\left[P(t') - P(t'-1)\right] \quad (3.3)$$

## Further Readings

*Futures market in general*

You can refer to [25] as a guide to futures market in general. This chapter also refers to this book largely. Furthermore, for those who want to learn about recent research on futures market in general, the book [3] is also available.

*Technical analysis*

[17] introduces many things about technical analysis carefully, from the historical processes of each method to practical methods. Refer to [1] as a specialized book for the description of actual techniques.

*Theories in general*

[18] is very beneficial for finance theories in general. You can refer to [15] and [16] for the stock market structure and market participants' behavior.

*Artificial market and econophysics*

The book [5] bearing the name 'artificial market' is beneficial for learning the artificial market. [19] can be a suitable guide to econophysics.

*Other*

The handbook of evolutionary economics authored by many of U-Mart project members is recommended as a book which describes the methods and concepts that are utilized in U-Mart as a whole, such as artificial markets and learning agents.

Glossary

| | |
|---|---|
| Contract | To make an agreement to settle. It indicates the establishment of a transaction. |
| Spot trading | Trading in which contracted transaction is carried out in short period of time. |
| Futures trading | Trading that a seller and buyer undertake to deliver a trading product at a certain future time at the price established at the present time. |
| Hedge (risk hedge) | To avert the future price volatility risks, lock in profits by selling spot products and buying futures products, or buying spot products and selling futures products. It is also referred to as 'hedge sale.' |
| Contract month | A due date that the actual product must be delivered. |
| Current delivery | A transaction having the due date of the end of the month. |
| Two-month delivery | A transaction having the due date at the end of the next month. |
| Future delivery | A transaction of which the due date is the most future in the market. |
| Long account | The promise to buy in futures trading. |
| Short account | The promise to sell in futures trading. |
| Contracts (open interest) | This indicates the transaction agreement before implementation in general without distinguishing buying or selling. |
| Partial contract | The spread between a long account and a short account. |
| Position | Partial contracts. This is called 'short position' when the long account is larger, and is called 'long position' when the short account is larger. |
| Closed trade | Trading that is opposite to the current position. Long position is placed when having the short position, and vice versa. |
| Closing out | To close out all the positions by conducting a closed trade. |
| Margin money | Money kept in the exchange as a resource for netting. Guarantee money. Money on deposit. |
| Mark-to-Market | To increase and decrease margin money balance by settling the profit and loss of all contracts, reflecting the daily price movement. |
| Candle chart | A chart that graphically shows the time series transition of opening price, closing price, high price, and low price. |
| Fundamentals | The fundamental economic conditions, such as GDP growth rate, interest rate, and earning rate. |
| Stop price | In a market which limits the price fluctuation band of the day in order to prevent investment overheating, when the price reaches the full limitation of fluctuation band, it is called the 'limit high.' 'Limit low' means the price fell off to the bottom of the limitation. |
| Morning session | Trading taken place in the morning. |

Afternoon session Trading taken place in the afternoon.

Opening auction The beginning of trading.

Close of the session The end of trading. The end of afternoon session means the end of the day.

Average buy To further buy positions when the price tends to fall off in order to get the average price down in the long positions that one owns.

Average sell To further sell positions when the price tends to rise in order to raise the average price in short positions one owns.

# Part II
# Application

# Chapter 4
# A Case of U-Mart Experiment by Human Agents

## 4.1 Introduction

Recently, an online investment with a low transaction fee has been popular for growing rate of Internet, and many people so-called a "private investor" have entered stock trading. Comparing to other western countries, Japan has a low percentage of direct finances in aggregate amount saved. In such a sense, this phenomenon may be what should be welcomed. However, it is true and regretful that there is a trend to have a fun with a money game being unable to appreciate the importance of production activities and productive technologies of manufacturing sectors. The U-Mart system has been developed for research, but also as a helpful educational tool for understanding financial futures market. Experimental participants are able to deepen understanding of futures market through a practical trading experience. However, the objective of the understanding of futures market does not aim for producing the winners in such a money game; rather, it aims for hoping and contributing to a healthy development and maturing of stock market. The U-Mart also includes such a meaning. Hence, this experiment is primarily conducted for the purpose of improving the students' understanding of futures market. In addition to this experiment, the experiment we conducted had another two objectives. The first objective was to examine what effects the availability of order book had on the humans' trading behavior as a trader. The second objective was to collect useful data such as environmental conditions for experiment in conducting the U-Mart experiment by humans. The experiment by humans, compared with that of the programmed machine trader, requires relatively high cost due to the necessity of preparation and restriction on experimental period. Therefore, determining the experimental conditions upon the start of the experiment of this sort needs careful consideration. The experiment this chapter introduces conducted at Kinki University in 2004 was conducted under the conditions improved based on the experience of the experiment conducted at Department of Economics of Osaka Sangyo University in 2002. The conditions were, needless to say, not to restrict the conditions for further experiment, but the data in the present experiment should be quite useful source for a ninety-minute lesson. Moreover, this chapter introduces the summary of necessary preparation for the participants since it should be useful for conducting a similar experiment. The participants are 17 students enrolled in Taniguchi's seminar course (humans) and a programmed machine to calculate the indicative price.

Regarding the U-Mart system, a new version was released in 2004 with the improved features. For clients, the user interface has been largely improved, and trading status can be shown to human traders more precisely than that of the first version. The amount of data that can be displayed also largely has increased, and subtle changes have been made so that the users can easily operate the displaying functions. Furthermore, Windows is added to the compatible OS of the server, which was only Linux in the old version, so the experiment could be conducted with ease. Moreover, the log data are outputted in csv format; this improvement facilitates data processing. Compared with the previous version of the U-Mart system, the operational procedures have dramatically been improved. We hope that this book encourages many to use the U-Mart system.

## 4.2 Objectives of Experiment

In addition to the students' understanding of futures market, the objectives of conducting the present experiment are the following.

1. To examine the influence of the availability of order book on the trading behaviors of market participants. That is, to examine what effects the availability of order book has on the order volume, execution volume, the number of orders, the number of executions, position control, realized profit and loss, etc of individual agents.
2. To preliminarily examine how the availability of order book influences the market as a whole.
3. To investigate the appropriate experimental conditions for the U-Mart experiments by humans through the preparation for the experiment.

## 4.3 Preparation: Learning of Futures Market and Pilot Experiment

Upon the conduct of the U-Mart experiment, the certain knowledge about the know-how of futures market and trading rules is required. As an educational tool, Chapter 3 of the current volume seems sufficient, and it can be used as students' self-study material. Since it includes references as well, it is recommended for further learning.

At the same time as the learning session of futures market, we conducted pilot experiments. Using the U-Mart system, the users can review the rules on futures market such as marking to the market, profit margin, position control, etc through

experiments; thus, the U-Mart is an effective educational material when used with Chapter 3. More specifically, during the two lessons in the spring semester, an experiment was conducted, and the data analysis of the experiment was assigned so that students could further their understanding of the rules and trading strategies. Moreover, a summer camp was held for intensive training. Additional two lessons of experiment were held during the fall semester. For students to internalize the knowledge they learned during the spring semester, sufficient time for *Itayose* was taken as much as they needed, so that they could consider their decisions after placing orders. In the first pilot experiment (September 16), the primary focus was on how to analyze the order book; in the second pilot experiment (September 30), the trading was performed by looking at only the chart without the order book.

## 4.4 Experimental Environment

### *4.4.1 Conditions for Trading*

Based on the findings from the preparation and pilot experiments, the conditions for the present experiment are determined as follows:

1. The *Itayose* trading session is held three times a day, and 20 seconds is given to each.
2. Total thirty-day futures market, namely ninety times of *Itayose* trading, is performed.
3. The actual period of time for the experiment is total forty minutes. (20 sec. $\times$ 3 + 20 sec.)$\times$ 30 days

A longer experiment, of course, can provide more data, but humans' attention span has its limitation. In the present experiment, 20 seconds is given to the *Itayose* session; it can be reduced up to about ten seconds. In the experiment in 2002, in fact, the time period for each *Itayose* was set as ten seconds, which was held eight times a day during 24 days of experiment. Moreover, in the open experiment, U-Mart 2004, the U-Mart project team held on September 2, 2004, with the 28 human participants from Osaka City University (Graduate School), Chuo University, and Kinki University, during the 20 days of futures trading, one experiment with twice of thirty-second *Itayose* a day and the other with ninety times of *Itayose,* each of which lasts one second were conducted.

### 4.4.2 Availability of Order Book

The 17 participants were assigned in two groups, group A (n=9) and group B (n=8). In the first experiment, we examined the case in which group A could see the order book, but group B could not. In the second experiment, the case in which group B could see the order book, but group A could not was examined. In the third experiment, we examined the case with the order book available for both groups, and the case with the order book unavailable for both groups was examined in the forth experiment. We used a machine agent to calculate the indicative price at the beginning of *Itayose*. This agent makes trading strategies in accordance with the information about the spread and stock, and the strategies include to increase bid quotation upon selling and to reduce asked quotation upon purchase to find out the bid and asked quotation.

### 4.4.3 Spot Price Data

We used J30 from Mainichi Newspapers Co., Ltd. that is equipped with the U-Mart system. It includes approximately 2,400 spot price data. In each experimental case, ninety times of *Itayose* are held with the data selected from the 2,400 spot price data. Table 4.1 summarizes the starting step of the data used in each case of the experiment as well as the date of experiment and the availability of the order book.

**Table 4.1** Experimental Environment for Each Case

| | Date | Steps of Spot Price J30 | Availability of Order Book |
|---|---|---|---|
| Case 1 | October 7 | 200 step | Group A with Order Book/Group B without Order Book |
| Case 2 | October 14 | 300step | Group A without Order Book/Group A with Order Book |
| Case 3 | October 21 | 600step | Both Groups with Order Book |
| Case 4 | October 28 | 500step | Both Groups without Order Book |

## 4.5 Results

### *4.5.1 Movement in Forward Price*

The price movements of all experimental cases are shown in Fig. 4.1, 4.2, 4.3, and 4.4. The experiment of Case 1 and 2 shows a downtrend; Case 3 shows an upward tendency at the end; Case 4 shows an erratic fluctuation. The range in price movements in Case 1, 2, and 4 is approximately 300 Japanese yen, and that of Case 3 is about 400 Japanese yen.

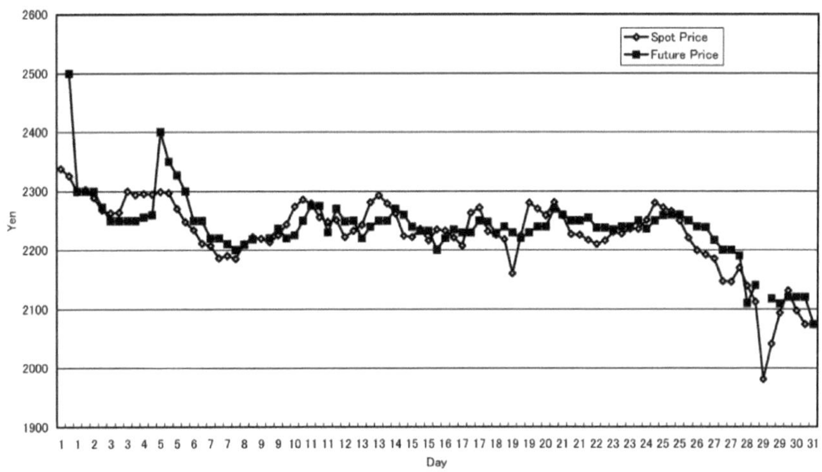


**Fig. 4.1** Case 1

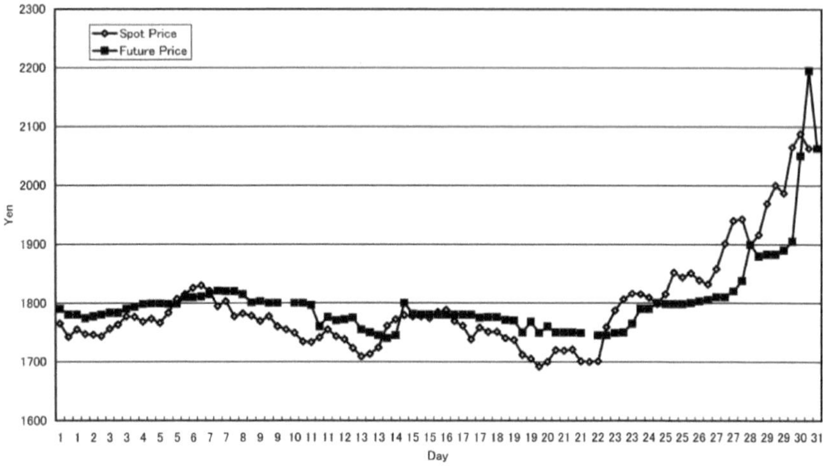


**Fig. 4.2** Case 2

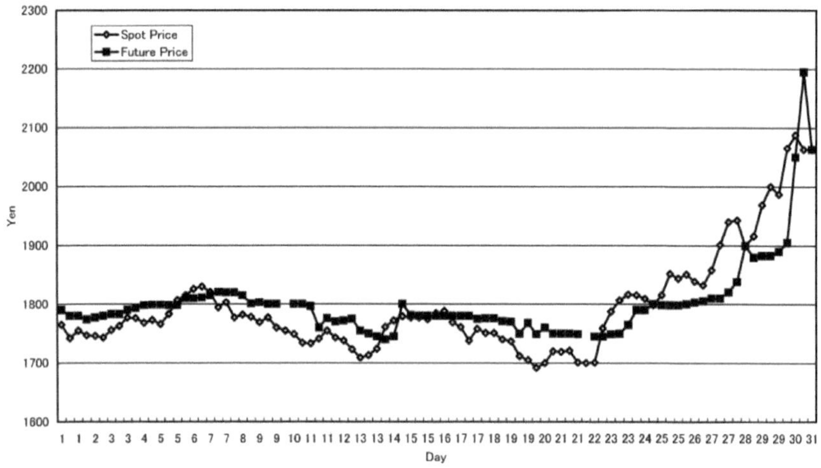


**Fig. 4.3** Case 3

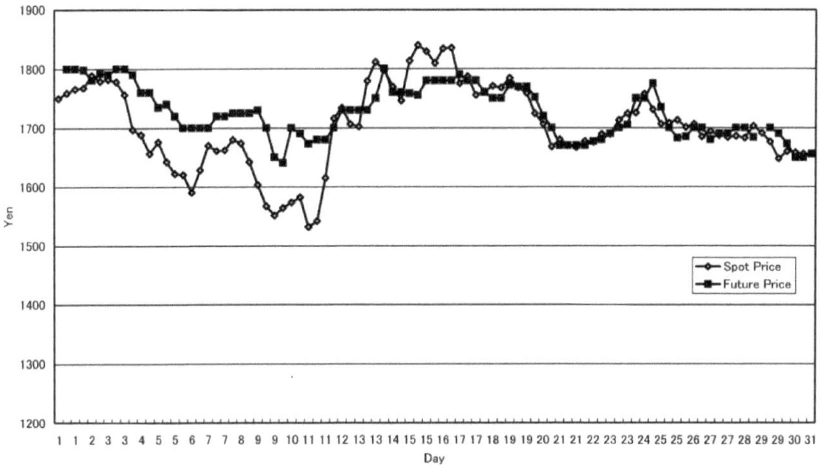


**Fig. 4.4** Case 4

## *4.5.2 Availability of Order Book and Execution Rate*

In terms of execution rate, the following two formulas are applied, and a hypothetical statistical test was employed for each at the significance level of 5%.

$$\text{Execution Rate based on the Execution Volume} = \text{Execution Volume}/\text{Order Volume}$$

$$\text{Execution Rate based on the Number of Executions} = \text{Number of Executions}/\text{Number of Orders}$$

It should be noted, however, that order volume is the sum of selling order volume and buying order volume and that the number of orders is the sum of the number of orders and the number of cancelling orders. The execution rate for each agent is shown in Table 4.2 and 4.3. In Table 4.3, one execution rate exceeds 1 (one) because it includes the execution in multiple *Itayose* sessions; the order volume was too large to be dealt in one *Itayose*, so the remaining order volume was processed in the next session.

Using these data, we employed one-way analysis of variance (ANOVA) for the execution rate with the availability of order book as the independent variable. That is, we employed the ANOVA test at the significant level of 5% for the following null hypothesis: "The experimental data for each group belong to the same population; that is, the availability of order book does not influence the execution rate." The result is shown in Table 4.4 and 4.5. A significant difference was found in the execution rate based on the number of executions, but as for the execution rate based on the execution volume, the obtained variance ratio was beyond the rejection range; thus, the null hypothesis was adopted. One of the reasons why no significant difference was found is that when the order book was available, the range in individual

**Table 4.2** The Execution Rate based on the Execution Volume

| Agent | With Order Book (Case 1 & 2) | Without Order Book (Case 1 & 2) | With Order Book (Case 3) | Without Order Book (Case 4) |
|---|---|---|---|---|
| h1 | 0.663 | 0.5 | 0.559 | 0.557 |
| h2 | 0.438 | 0.255 | 0.432 | 0.142 |
| h3 | 0.563 | 0.442 | 0.523 | 0.472 |
| h4 | 0.312 | 0.274 | 0.577 | 0.350 |
| h5 | 0.216 | 0.147 | 0.253 | 0.482 |
| h6 | 0.380 | 0.413 | 0.414 | 0.591 |
| h7 | 0.833 | 0.466 | 0.349 | 0.371 |
| h8 | 0.596 | 0.460 | 0.204 | 0.566 |
| h9 | 0.508 | 0.242 | 0.287 | 0.191 |
| h10 | 0.446 | 0.339 | 0.425 | 0.364 |
| h11 | 0.526 | 0.428 | 0.783 | 0.494 |
| h12 | 0.353 | 0.405 | 0.177 | 0.746 |
| h13 | 0.418 | 0.265 | 0.387 | 0.402 |
| h14 | 0.481 | 0.552 | 0.458 | 0.781 |
| h15 | 0.158 | 0.103 | 0.234 | 0.338 |
| h16 | 0.683 | 0.287 | 0.505 | 0.283 |
| h17 | 0.092 | 0.379 | 0.472 | 0.420 |
| Mean | 0.451 | 0.350 | 0.414 | 0.444 |
| Variance | 0.037 | 0.016 | 0.024 | 0.030 |

agents' order volume was large, so the variance in such a case became large as well. In other words, the availability of order book seems to have little influence on the order volume, but it seems to an effective determining factor of the timing of placing an order within the 20 seconds of *Itayose* so that the order can achieve its execution.

Moreover, Fig. 4.5 and 4.6 with the vertical axis designated as "with order book" and the horizontal axis as "without order book" show the execution rate of each agent.

In cases of that the order book is available to all participants (Case 3) and that the order book is unavailable to all participants (Case 4), the execution rate for the case with the available order book was lower than that of unavailable order book. The price movements and differences in individual agents' external environment may contribute to this result; however, the actual causes cannot be determined from this experiment. The apparent influence of the availability of the order book on the whole market was not obtained in this experiment.

**Table 4.3** The Execution Rate based on the Number of Executions

| Agent | With Order Book (Case 1 & 2) | Without Order Book (Case 1 & 2) | With Order Book (Case 3) | Without Order Book (Case 4) |
|---|---|---|---|---|
| h1 | 0.718 | 0.526 | 0.536 | 0.586 |
| h2 | 0.474 | 0.408 | 0.538 | 0.293 |
| h3 | 0.573 | 0.517 | 0.567 | 0.514 |
| h4 | 0.462 | 0.368 | 0.714 | 1.091 |
| h5 | 0.216 | 0.195 | 0.264 | 0.493 |
| h6 | 0.404 | 0.396 | 0.400 | 0.607 |
| h7 | 0.789 | 0.600 | 0.350 | 0.595 |
| h8 | 0.592 | 0.460 | 0.229 | 0.566 |
| h9 | 0.536 | 0.271 | 0.452 | 0.266 |
| h10 | 0.471 | 0.364 | 0.472 | 0.370 |
| h11 | 0.537 | 0.401 | 0.774 | 0.499 |
| h12 | 0.444 | 0.392 | 0.319 | 0.737 |
| h13 | 0.491 | 0.328 | 0.454 | 0.405 |
| h14 | 0.547 | 0.515 | 0.484 | 0.771 |
| h15 | 0.225 | 0.143 | 0.417 | 0.349 |
| h16 | 0.706 | 0.336 | 0.524 | 0.305 |
| h17 | 0.615 | 0.446 | 0.513 | 0.440 |
| Mean | 0.518 | 0.392 | 0.471 | 0.523 |
| Variance | 0.023 | 0.014 | 0.020 | 0.043 |

**Table 4.4** The Analysis-of Variance Table of Execution Rate based on the Execution Volume (Case 1 & 2)

| | Variables | Degrees of Freedom | Variance | Observed Variance Ratio | F Value (Significant Level $p<.05$) |
|---|---|---|---|---|---|
| Availability of Order Book | 0.086 | 1 | 0.086 | 3.266 | 4.149 |
| Difference | 0.844 | 32 | 0.026 | | |
| Total | 0.930 | 33 | | | |

**Table 4.5** The Analysis-of-Variance Table of Execution Rate based on the Number of Execution (Case 1 & 2)

| | Variables | Degrees of Freedom | Variance | Observed Variance Ratio | F Value (Significant Level $p<.05$) |
|---|---|---|---|---|---|
| Availability of Order Book | 0.134 | 1 | 0.134 | 7.177 | 4.149 |
| Difference | 0.597 | 32 | 0.019 | | |
| Total | 0.730 | 33 | | | |

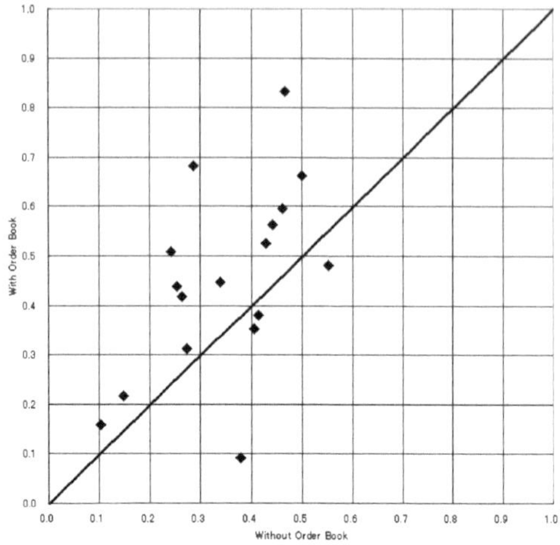


**Fig. 4.5** Individual Agents' Execution Rate based on the Execution Volume

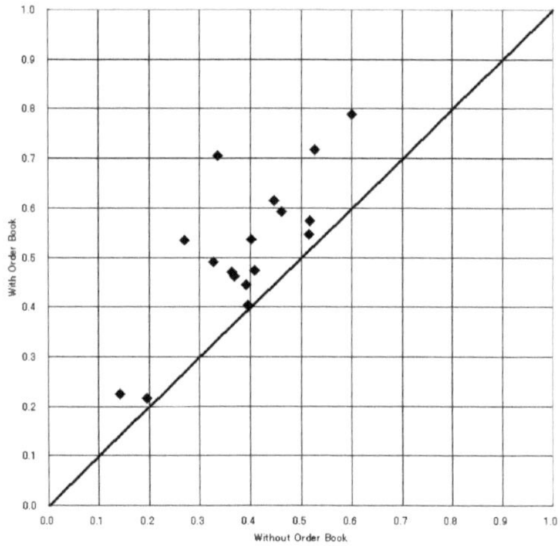


**Fig. 4.6** Individual Agents' Execution Rate based on the Number of Execution

### *4.5.3 Changes in Order Volume and the Number of Orders*

As shown in Fig. 4.7, in later experiments, larger order volume was found; the order volume in Case 4 was about 3.1 times as much as that of Case 1. As for the number of orders, no large increase was found as shown in Fig. 4.8; the average number of orders per agent was from 1.2 to 1.6 times during each *Itayose* session. From the result, it can be said that, for the humans' orders, the frequency of orders do not depend on the trading conditions. In fact, our observation tells that during the 20 seconds of *Itayose*, many agents watch the run of events and tend to place orders in the last few seconds. In terms of the order volume, the repetition of experiments seems to facilitate the participants' learning of it. In this respect, it can be said that their learning curve does not still reach the stable stage.

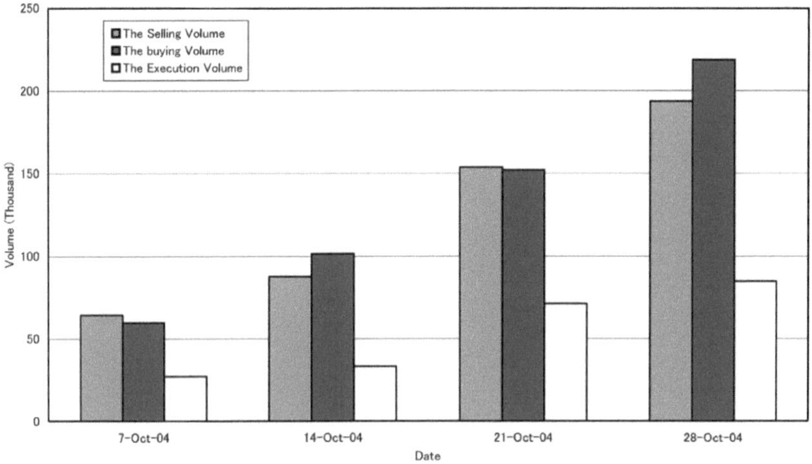


**Fig. 4.7** The Order Volume and Execution Volume

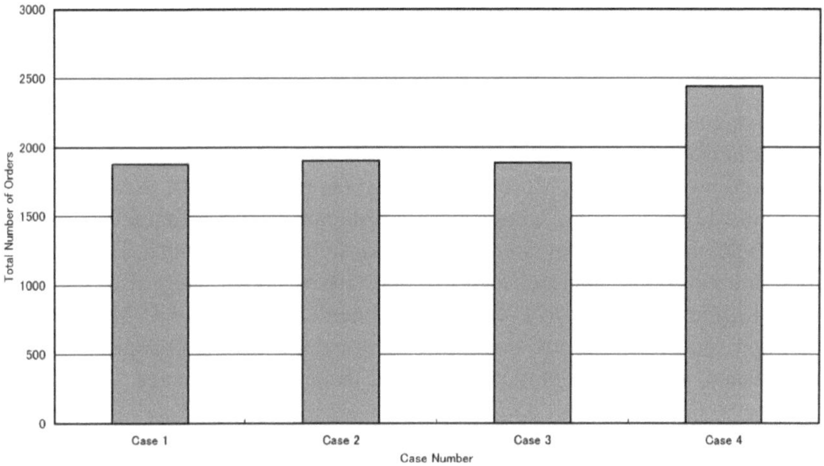


**Fig. 4.8** The Number of Orders

### *4.5.4 Changes in Position*

Most agents were able to learn the position control through the pilot experiments for learning; nonetheless, given the variances in Case 1, 2, 3, and 4 were 0.049, 0.047, 0.159, and 0.069 respectively, the position control in Case 3 seemed quite difficult. The dramatic movement in price in Case 3 may account for the difficulty (See Fig. 4.9).

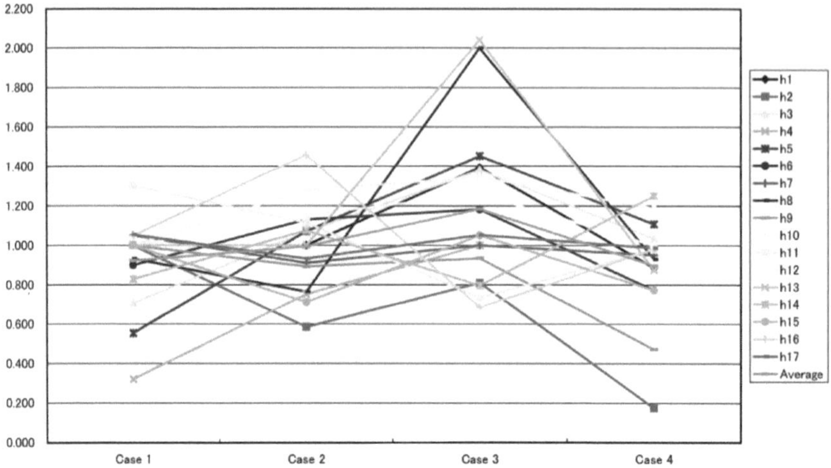


**Fig. 4.9** Agents' Position Control (Selling Volume/Buying Volume)

### *4.5.5 Changes in Realized Profit and Loss*

The individual realized profit and loss for each case is summarized in Fig. 4.10. The present experiment shows that the availability of order book does not influence the realized profit and loss. More interestingly, the realized profit and loss depends on individual human agents' characters. The amount of loss of agent h11 and h16 is sometimes large, but they sometimes make tremendous profits. They read the market situations and take a chance like a "market player." They also reached an excellent achievement in the U-Mart 2004, open experiment of U-Mart.[1] On the other hand, quite a few agents, though they learned the trading strategies, could not take a chance, and resulted in more loss rather than profit on average.

## 4.6 Conclusion

We conducted the experiment in 2002, using the first version of the U-Mart system, to examine the influence of the availability of order book on the contracted rate, but no significant difference was found in the result. The present experiment basically shares the same objectives with that of 2002; however, the availability of order book brought about the significant difference in the contracted rate based on the number of contract. One of the reasons can be the improvement of the U-Mart system. The new version, compared with the first version, not only is more use-friendly, but also has the improved interface. In addition to the graphic display of order book found in

[1] Refer to Kazuhisa Taniguchi and Yohei Noguchi's "A Report of U-Mart 2004 Experiment" Report presented at the Ninth Annual Conference of the Japan Association for Evolutionary Economics.

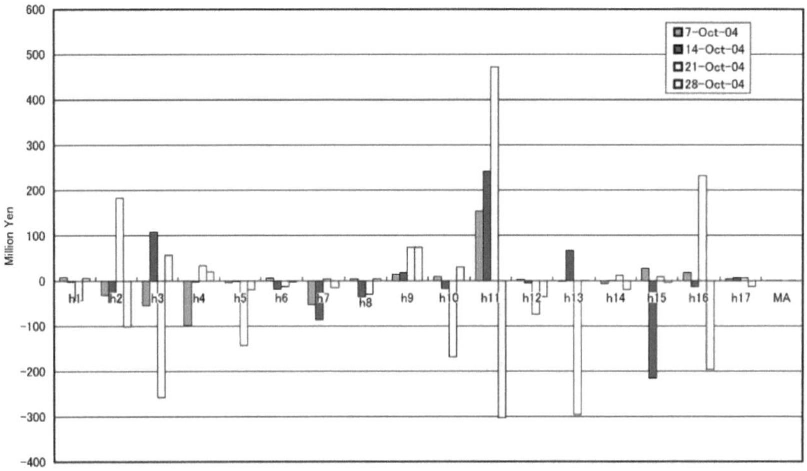


**Fig. 4.10** Agents' Realized Profit and Loss

the first version, the display using digital data just like the one in actual transaction is used in the new version. Being able to display the *Itayose* information almost in real time is a great improvement as well. The second reason is that the learning session before the experiment is improved. For instance, upon the transaction, learners can order and cancel as many times as needed until they are satisfied with their decision, and this sufficient time allocated for Itayose seems to contribute to the result. The third reason is that in the experiment of 2002, 20 of random-type software agents participated, so the difference in agent type (i.e. human vs. machine) seems to be a contributing factor.[2]

However, despite the fact that the two experiments largely differ in the versions of the U-Mart systems and participating agents, the order volume and order frequency show similarities. Moreover, the realized profit and loss and position control also do not show great differences. The appearance of excellent traders like a "speculator" is also a common phenomenon. Those seem to depend on humans' characteristics, but the apparent causes are still unanswered; therefore, further research is needed.

The U-Mart system, which is versatile and can be used in both research and education, is a virtual stock market simulator for experiment. With regard to research, many have already been reported. Also it is used in engineering education through the development of programming software. Nevertheless, since the experiment in which humans participate is the costly alternative, the obtained data are limited. The practical use in future education should accumulate the data from experiment; thus, further know-how is expected to be obtained.

---

[2] The agent is able to place an order around the spot price randomly and to create the breath of market.

Reference Material: Report Assignment

Analyzing the data obtained through the two U-Mart experiments conducted on May $13^{th}$ and $20^{th}$, summarize your own transaction result in accord with the following items.

1. Check the numbers of market order and limit order.
2. Regarding each of market orders and limit orders, calculate the percentage of the sell contract volume and order volume after evaluating them.
3. Likewise, calculate the percentage of the buy contract volume and sell order volume.
4. Make a graph of time series that of the sum of position and the sum of buy position.
5. Make a time-series graph of unsettled profits and surplus.
6. Present settled profits.
7. Through the two experiments conducted this time, analyze the cause and reason of winning or loosing in the transaction in your own way.
8. Express your own impressions for these experiments.

Questionnaire Result after Experiments

The following questions were asked after the experiments. Fig. 4.11, 4.12 shows the questionnaire results.

1. Where the order book was unavailable, did chart information help you to decide the order price?
2. Where the order book was unavailable, did chart information help you to decide the order volume?
3. Where the order book was available, did chart information help you to decide the order price?
4. Where the order book was available, did chart information help you to decide the order volume?
5. Where the order book could be referred, did the order book help you to decide the order price?
6. Where the order book could be referred, did the order book help you to decide the order volume?
7. Have your understanding toward futures market deepened by participating in the U-Mart experiment?
8. The time interval for one *Itayose* trading session is 20 seconds, how do you feel about this time interval?
9. The period of futures market are 30 days, how do you feel about this period?
10. The actual experiment duration is 40 minutes, how do you feel about this duration?

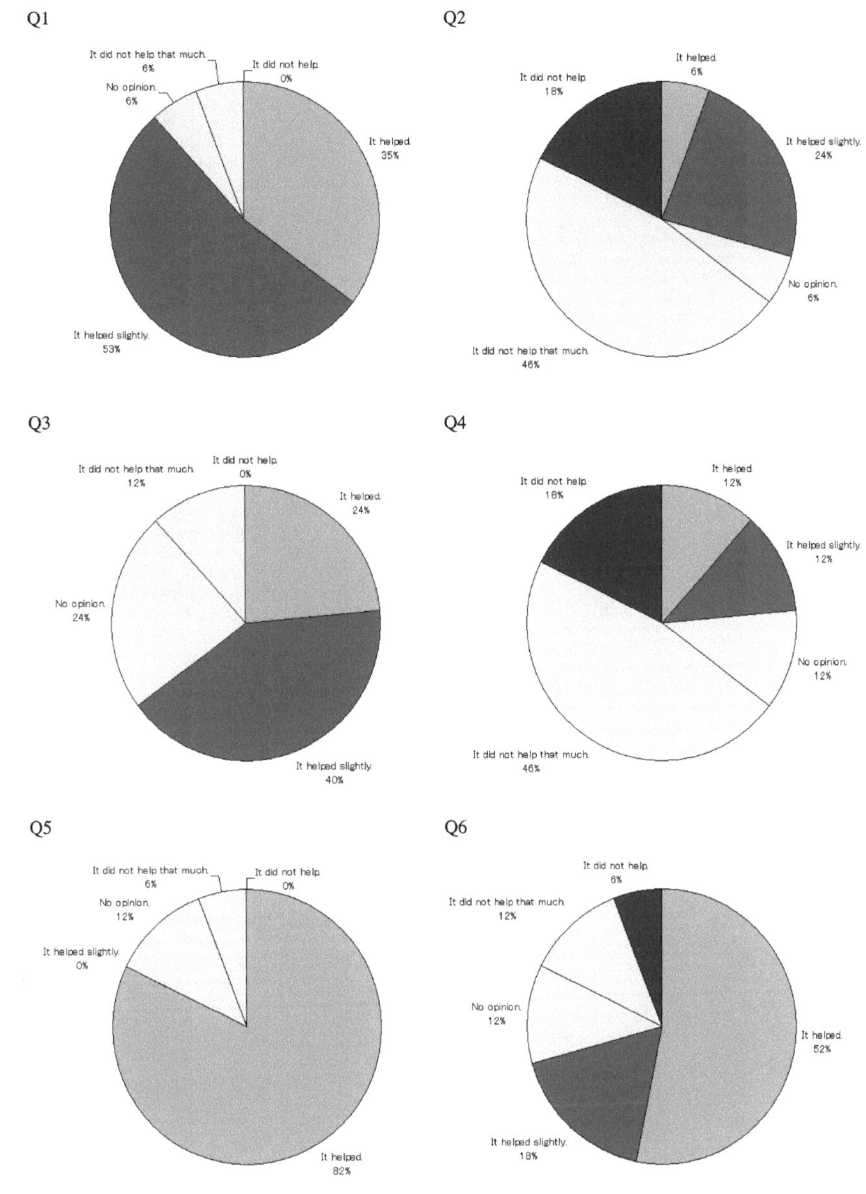


**Fig. 4.11** Questionnaire Results (1)

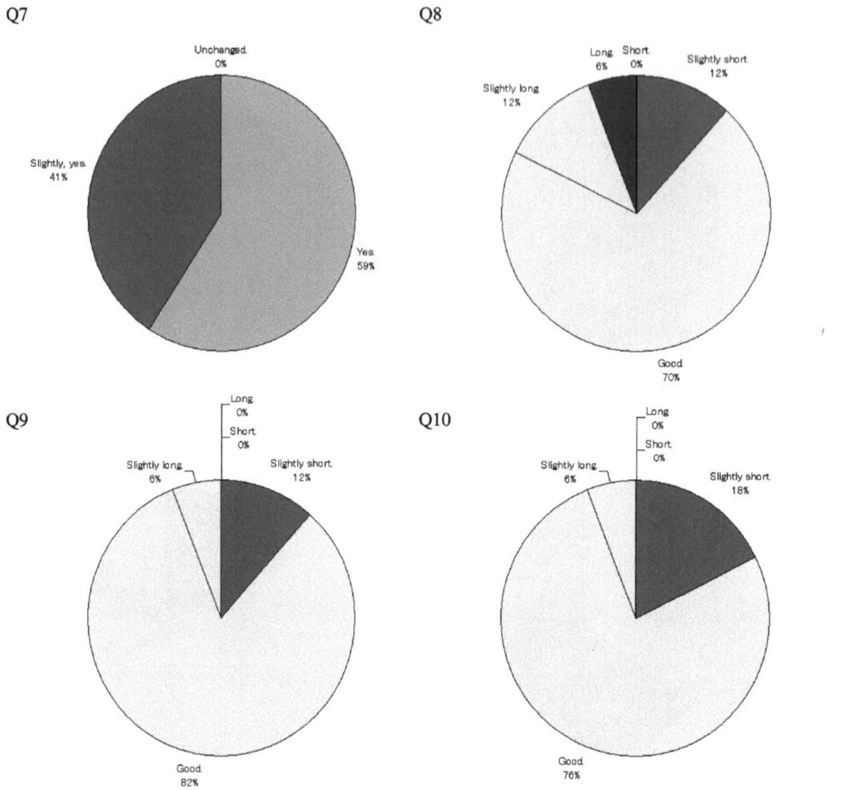


**Fig. 4.12** Questionnaire Results (2)

# Chapter 5
# Statistical Analysis of U-Mart Experiments by Humans

## 5.1 Introduction

Differing from the concept of an 'error' in the domain of natural science, a societal phenomenon consists of various substances and its transactions which are fundamental. Sadly, it is very difficult for we humans to understand all diversity as it is, so we need to simplify them to a state that we can understand them, without loosing its characteristics. By doing this, diversity is resolved to 'principle,' and based on that principle, it becomes possible to mention unmeasured substances and to predict the future. 'Statistics' is a method to do this. Although the same experimental and research results are obtained, if the statistical viewpoint is missed, we are obsessed with individual phenomenon that is no more than a part of diversity, and it prevents us from finding out the existing underlying principle.

Certainly, the error that principle arrows in a domain of natural science (e.g. classical mechanics or chemistry) has been elaborated to the extent these days to conclude that there is no requirement for the need of statistics. In an usual experiment or observation, it never happens that the theoretical figure might be missed even once in a hundred times (recall the theoretical concept of falsification proposed by Karl Popper). However, in the scientifically-undeveloped academic domains like medical science or social science, statistics accompanied by experimental plans and examinations are essential.

Additionally, despite of physical smallness of humans, each individual human has vast amounts of parameters. Therefore, even if in a planned experimental scene, it is difficult to substantially stabilize the variables, other than those that can be controlled. Consequently, statistics is required to pool and handle all of them as error.

Now, in social science, where statistics can be utilized based on obtained data setting in an experimental scene especially with human subjects, the following points will be described step by step in this chapter, regarding what kind of procedures are required and how analysis should be done.

(1) What (conceptual) preparation is required?

(2) Experimental plan and reminders assuming statistical processing
(3) Data extraction with Excel
(4) Simple statistical analysis with Excel
(5) Somewhat full-fledged statistical analysis using statistical packages like SPSS
(6) Various types of statistical methods applicable to analyze the U-Mart experiment subjects

## 5.2 What (Conceptual) Preparation is Required?

### *5.2.1 Observation and Experiment*

Where an intended phenomenon is not under our control, namely, where we cannot control the occurrence time of phenomenon, and where it is impossible to configure various parameters associated with its occurrence, we are able to only 'observe' such a phenomenon. In the domain of social science, this is equivalent to such phenomena as massive group behavior, and a phenomenon that is accompanied by somewhat 'destruction (or a noninvertible load for biological objects).'

When we try to obtain new knowledge (e.g. a new rule) by observation, the first difficulty is to specify which parameter is the cause. It is impossible to confirm the cause when a certain phenomenon occurs with several parameters changed simultaneously. In addition, there is a possibility that the temporal change of a relevant object by the observation time itself also works as one of the parameters. For these difficulties, increasing the observation objects can bring a solution. In other words, the particular difference among the objects can be removed by seizing the opportunity when the respective parameters change independently in order to compare to a previous observation, and additionally, observing another object separately from the previous observation. However, it is nearly impossible to expect that such a phenomenon occurs according to a sequence and or format that we anticipated, in addition, we are limited by time.

On the other hand, through experiments, we are able to overcome the above mentioned difficulties more easily. Namely, regarding the target phenomenon, conducting an experiment by fixing all the phenomenon parameters other than the parameters to be focused on can attribute the cause of obtained results dispersion to the transition of its parameter (as described precisely later, actually, the definite results cannot be obtained by only one experiment since the experimental objects have a difference, or the difference is due to repetition between the same objects (in general, this is viewed as 'noise' or 'error')).

However, that is not to say that it is always the best to conduct an experiment under any circumstances. This is especially true because where humans are adopted as experimental subjects, the restrictions on parameters cause experimental subjects to be put under extraordinary conditions. This reason alone might cause different behavior of experimental subjects of what is normal. Stated another way, the following fundamental concept of an experiment certainly has its weakness: human behavior is the result from the interaction (or cross-interaction) of various parameters, and the discussion is allowed by taking out particular parameters. Still, as long as many things exist that we cannot obtain by only observation (cannot obtain within the time we expect), we need to benefit from conducting experiments to grasp some sort of rules in human behavior. By doing so, we are able to understand the meaning of human behavior under various circumstances, and aim at predicting human behavior in the unknown scene.

### *5.2.2 Description Statistics and Experimental Plan*

Statistics include the following two concepts in broad terms: description statistics and hypothesis test. To conduct the effective hypothesis test, particularly, a thorough experimental plan is required in advance. With that, the same results can be obtained with less effort by adjusting the parameters (the number of subjects and repetition). To put it the other way around, although an experiment is conducted without designing a plan minutely, it could be that only slight results are obtained for the time spent on the experiment itself or costs. This chapter mainly discusses how to design the experimental plan.

Description statistics, just as described by its name, is statistics that describes obtained raw data intensively. In particular, it tries to use well-known indexes such as ‘average rate,’ ‘standard deviation,’ or ‘mode’ in order to learn the characteristics of data (or the universe that is the source of data). These statistics can summarize the characteristics of data; however, it is difficult to step up a discussion about its meaning. To be more precise, although where the average and standard deviation of a certain observed value differ regarding two samples that have differences on a particular parameter axis, those indexes are description indexes for respective samples. Based on this information only, these statistics are unable to describe which parameter affects observed data (or, which parameter does not affect observed data), and what kind of influence observed data comes under.

## 5.3 Experimental Plan and Reminders Assuming Statistical Processing

As already mentioned, to conduct an effective analysis, it is required to develop the experimental plan deliberately before the actual experiment as subjects is conducted. Specifically, there are some points that should be considered as follows.

(1) What kind of statistical processing is conducted, and for what purpose? (Refer to each processing method shown later)
(2) How many experimental subjects can be gathered?

(3) How many times can one experimental subject undergo an experiment?
(4) How much time can be spent for a single experiment?
(5) Can multiple subjects undergo the experiment simultaneously? Or, are only the individual experiments conducted?

Suppose, for example, an experiment is conducted on two factors, A and B. The factor A is "those subjects who learned a certain strategy in advance, and those who did not." The factor B is "those subjects who are given 'all' particular additional information, those who are given 'some' of additional information, and those who are not given additional information." At this time, there are two factors and the numbers of each level are two and three, respectively. In this case, to observe the interactions of factor A and B, it is desirable to divide the subjects into six groups, and each group has approximately 25 subjects. Hence, a total of 150 subjects are needed in the case of this experiment. At a minimum, each group needs 8 subjects. That means approximately 50 subjects are required. A small number of subjects might bring the statistical analysis result that "analysis has not shown that this result is out of error range (because of the lack of adequate data)," and in many cases, it results in just obtaining the result of "non-significant." However, we need to take notice that this case has not shown that there is no difference; rather, the result shows no more than the result of "no-opinion" as shown by the expression "non-significant."

Increasing the number of factors and levels allows investigating a variety of influences with one experiment, and interactions can also be examined. However, a large number of subjects should be required because the required number of subjects is proportional to the number that is multiplied the level of each factor.

Obviously, the U-Mart experiment using an ordinary server can target multiple subjects. However, where the eye mark recorder is used for measurement regarding, for example, on which part of data a subject focuses (unless several eye mark recorders are ready to be prepared); the experimental form must be the individual an experiment. In such a case, adopting hundreds of subjects is very realistically difficult.

Additionally, where we desire to prove that our target matter is not influenced by the parameters other than those are configured as an experimental setting, for example, to prove that the U-Mart experimental result does not depend on a particular time series used in the relevant experiment, adequate numbers of time series should be utilized in order to flatten those parameter fluctuations statistically. To realize this, multiple experiments should definitely be conducted.

On the other hand, where the experiment is conducted over multiple times and identical experimental subjects participate in the experiment over and over, there is a possibility that the subject's condition itself might change in every experiment due to the "practice effect." Apart from an experiment that sets the practice effect itself as a parameter, a new subject should be adopted every time an experiment is conducted, or another experiment should be conducted preliminarily to show that the relevant experiment is independent of the practice effect.

Similarly, in laboratory experiments, the experimental conditions should be fixed wherever possible trying to prevent the subjects from coming under influences of the parameters other than the parameters that could be changed (e.g., the size of computer display, operation speed, brightness, the software version used by subject, whether subjects are acquaintances, whether the experiment is conducted as a part of classes or just collecting volunteer subjects, whether a reward is paid or not, whether there is some kind of prize for the final remarks or not).

## 5.4 Data Extraction with Excel

When processing obtained data in a some sort of statistical way, the processing work can be easy by changing the data format into the Excel file format.

Excel itself has an analysis tool for statistical analysis, but moreover, many statistical packages such as SPSS and so on are able to load an Excel file directly. Additionally, upon inputting data, the line column (length and width) and the direction of input line are designated in many statistical packages. In such a case, Excel becomes very useful in sorting data or converting the line columns in length and width.

Whatever the format of the original data is, data can be read by Excel if each data is converted into the CSV format that separates each data with ‘,’ (comma). Furthermore, even if data is saved in other file format than CSV format, selecting ‘Separation’ in ‘Data’ on the menu bar allows handling data as similar data as what is separated with the CSV format using separators and any digit number. All data obtained by U-Mart experiments is provided with this CSV format. However, the amount of data might exceed the Excel’s data-handling capacity when the numerous amounts of data are obtained. If this is the case, the data format should be changed from the beginning in order to enable the packaged software to read the data.

## 5.5 Simple Statistical Analysis with Excel

Excel has a standard analysis tool. Although this tool is not preinstalled at the default, it can be added anytime you like as an optional tool. The following functions are provided by the analysis tool of Excel for statistical processing.

- Various description statistics
- $t$-test
- Dispersion analysis for one factor
- Regression analysis and Multi-regression analysis

With t-test and dispersion analysis for one factor, this analysis tool can easily be utilized particularly for simple an experimental plan. This analysis tool can conduct multi-regression analysis as well as simple regression analysis, even if the number of parameters is multiple. However, the degree of variable is just the first order; no multi-regression analysis on multiple dimension more than second order can be conducted. In addition, it is possible to conduct more complicated computing of statistical processing by utilizing the functions such as macro language and Excel solver add in. Statistical analysis using Excel is an efficient method where learning statistics itself in addition (because users can process data confirming what kind of computing is done). However, where only the analysis result is required, it is more effective to utilize statistical packages introduced from following.

## 5.6 Somewhat Full-Fledged Statistical Analysis with SPSS

Statistical processing of SPSS depends on the package installed in a computer; however, adding one or two optional packages to the basic system allows SPSS to conduct major part of statistical processing just like the one used in analyzing U-Mart experiments. SPSS is a convenient tool particularly for dispersion analysis having a large numbers of factors, factor analysis, and principle component analysis. These analyses can be conducted by using only Excel, however, using SPSS-like tools provide for speedy processing. Additionally, when it occurs sometimes during an experiment that a value is missed, SPSS can specify what kind of processing needs to be conducted from the menu.

The old type of statistical packages that are embedded in such large computer systems are required to learn a description language, whereas the packages for recent PCs or WSs provide the graphical menu that allows users to conduct most analyses. As described as follows, however, a deliberate experimental plan must be designed in advance to conduct such statistical processing. With that, SPSS should be utilized after fully examining what kind of object is analyzed, and what kind of processing should be conducted. It should be mentioned that lack of preparation might lead to wasting time on repeating unnecessary experiments because of the irrelevant interpretation of the result outputted, or because no significant results could be obtained at all.

**Typical statistical processing method applicable to U-Mart experiment by subjects and the example of experimental plan**
**[Quantitative data and qualitative data]**

The data that is utilized in statistical processing (or it can be replaced by 'data that is measured') can be divided into two kinds, "Quantitative data" and "Qualitative data." In the U-Mart experiment, qualitative data is an index that indicates not only item numbers or sequences but also the actual quantity such as the number of transactions during the experiment, trading price per one transaction, or gained profit. In other words, it is an index like 3 that is one times three, or 10 that is five times two. On the other hand, qualitative data is an index that indicates item numbers like genders or grades of subjects, or the degree of maturity (of course grade two is not grade one times two). These indexes include such a meaning as an item number; however, such indexes are difficult to utilize directly for analysis as an index.

Since each statistical method has been developed for quantitative data and qualitative data respectively, users need to select their own statistical methods after confirming the data format for their analysis target data.

## 5.7 Various Types of Statistical Methods Applicable to Analyze the U-Mart Experiment

### *5.7.1 ANOVA (Analysis of Variance)*

(Example 1) Does the availability of order book have an affect on subjects behavior?

'The availability of order book' is set as a parameter. 'The price won finally,' 'transaction frequency,' and 'trading volume per one transaction' are set as measurements.

(Example 2) Does the degree of maturity have an affect on subject's behavior?

'Professionals,' 'Long-term students 'and 'Newcomers' are set as parameters. The same measurements with Example 1 are adopted.

(Example 3) As is the cases with Example 1 and 2, where the same indexes are used as a measurement, those indexes can be organized with two factors (First factor: 2 levels; Second factor: 3 levels). Organizing the indexes allows finalizing the experiment at one time. Not only that, the interaction can be examined, for example like on the following point, "professionals' measurements are influenced by the availability of the order book, but have no influence on beginners."

### *5.7.2 Regression Analysis*

(Example) How is the contract rate determined by 'transaction frequency,' 'types of strategy,' and 'the number of participants'?

Where an index that is always measurable is $x_1 \sim x_n$ and an index that is expected to be measured is $y$, this analysis method tries to obtain the estimated index for unknown $y$ from the data of $x_1 \sim x_n$ that is given, by expressing $y$ as the polynomial expression of $x_1 \sim x_n$.

### 5.7.3 Factor Analysis

(Example) Based on different behavior among subjects (measurable indexes such as 'transaction frequency,' 'an order price per one time,' and 'contract success rate'), this analysis method derives the factor structure existing behind such behavior.

The factor structure is defined as, for example, the above mentioned various measurable indexes are actually derived from only some (essential) factors that are not measured (if the factors are multiple, those factors are independent and in orthogonal relation).

As an often cited example, based on the measured remarks of subjects that are 'English,' 'Mathematics,' and 'National language,' this analysis method finds out independent factors existing behind the remarks such as the 'humanity factor' and the 'science factor.'

### 5.7.4 Quantification Theory

(Example) With regard to data having quantitative indexes, "Hayashi's quantification theory" represented by I, II, III, and IV can plot the relationship between each item on a two-dimensional plane, and can draw the expression that gives the expect index of measurements consisting of the combination of item numbers.

## 5.8 Details of Respective Statistical Analysis Methods

### 5.8.1 Description of Analysis of Variance

Analysis of variance is a method that examines whether the configured parameter values have an affect on the measurements by investigating its variance ratio. More specifically, in the case of analysis of variance on one factor having three levels is shown as follows.

Factor A: The effect of education

- A1: The subjects who got course credits with excellent results after taking a one-year U-Mart class.
- A2: The subjects who did not attend the one-year U-Mart class and could not get course credits.
- A3: The subjects who plan to attend the U-Mart class that will be held in the next semester.

Suppose, the groups from A1 to A3 have 20 subjects each. The final price of U-Mart is considered simply as a measurement.

Judging from the factor conditions, it is obviously impossible that an identical subject is included in two groups. In this case, if there is no effect by factor A and no noise is observed, all the measurements must be equivalent to the overall average index of the data of the 60 subjects, $X_{ij}$. The problem is what kind of cause makes respective data deviate from this overall average index.

If there is some sort of influence on factor A, each data of the A1 average, A2 average, and A3 average must adequately differ from the overall average index. As the standard to judge "being adequately different," when comparing the total variation that subtracts the overall average from each data and the factor variation that subtracts the overall average from each level average, it is concluded that factor A affects the measurements if the percentage of factor variation to total variation (dispersion rate) is above a certain level. To judge whether a certain dispersion rate is significant, it can be found by running the dispersion rate with the $F$ distribution chart based on the degree of freedom.

The same is true in the case of two factors or more, if both factors A and B do not affect the measurements and no noise is observed, all the data of all the groups must be equivalent to the same index with the overall average. The problem is how to examine whether the variation of factor A is significant enough when compared to the total variation, in addition, whether the variation of factor B is significant enough when compared to the total variation.

If the result, the influence of each factor, obtained by using the statistical analysis tools such as Excel or SPSS where the probability is smaller than 5%-level or 1%-level, it can be viewed that there seems to be an influence (this means where there is no factor influence at all, the probability that the percentage of factor variation becomes significant is xxx %. Hence, the smaller the index, the more it cannot be viewed as having no influence.).

## *5.8.2 Description of Multi-Regression Analysis*

The following variables are independent variables (parameters that are always measurable):

$x_1$ : Initial price
$x_2$ : Number of participants
$x_3$ : Average order volume per one time
$x_4$ : Broad type of strategy taken
Induced variable (index expected to measure):
$y$ : Contract rate

This analysis method can analyze data with regard to on which independent variable the contract rate mainly depends, and what relationship these variable have (or do not have) in a numerical sense.

In this experimental plan, since $x_2$ is given the number of participants as a parameter, multiple experiments are needed to be conducted for this plan by changing the number of participants. Therefore, it should be mentioned that an extremely long time is required for the entire experiment (as mentioned already, new experimental subjects are needed in each experiment in order to remove the influence of practice effect of subjects).

### 5.8.3 Description of Factor Analysis

Variables measured: $x_1$ and $x_2$

$$x_1 = a_1 \times \alpha + b_1 \times \beta + e_1$$

$$x_2 = a_2 \times \alpha + b_2 \times \beta + e_2$$

(Here, each of $\alpha$ and $\beta$ is assumed as a factor that is orthogonal to each other.)

The indexes like $x_1$ and $x_2$ that are actually measured are viewed as what has been synthesized by the particular coefficients for the factors of $\alpha$ and $\beta$ which form the structure behind such indexes. With that, those measurement items having complicated correlation to each other can be reduced to more primitive factors, so that the system structure under consideration can be explored.

### 5.8.4 Description of Quantitative Theory

This theory is a method that applies such analyses as analysis of variance, multi-regression analysis, and factor analysis to categorical data. This theory requires a somewhat advanced mathematical structure, but upon using this theory with the interpretation of results, there is no problem with viewing this theory as analysis for categorical data.

# Chapter 6
# Possibility and Meaning of the U-Mart

## 6.1 Introduction

Through the Practice section, you have been able to understand how the U-Mart system works and what kind of experiments and experiences are available. At the end of this book, this chapter overviews the possibility and meaning of the U-Mart study.

The U-Mart project is a study project that aims for developing new research tools for economics utilizing computer technologies. A variety of such studies have been done. Those studies are generally called simulation. It has been a while since the effectiveness of simulation methods was pointed out in the study of economic phenomenon as a result of complicated societal interactions. A cellular automaton had been regarded as a dominant method for a period of time, which was actually a highly inadequate method, setting its principled possibility aside. For social sciences, the cellular automaton had only a metaphorical meaning in a significant abstraction level, except that it can easily give a graphic representation of computing results.

On the other hand, as you have already realized, U-Mart has been successful in creating a condition having hardly any difference with the participation in real market. Breaking away from a mere figurative phase, the U-Mart has already come close to the point that it can serve for re-designing the actual market system and realizing a new market. The appearance of such a test-bed carries a potential to innovate economics study and jumps to a new stage. This chapter examines the research program of economics toward a new breakthrough.

## 6.2 A Short History of Economics

To consider the actual state of economics and look toward the future, it is necessary to review the history of economics briefly. The history of economics can broadly

**Table 6.1** Three stages of economics

| Classifications | Ages | Mainstream schools | Main methods |
|---|---|---|---|
| First stage | $19^{th}$ century | Classical economics | literary description |
| Second stage | $20^{th}$ century | Neoclassical economics | use of mathematics |
| Third stage | $21^{st}$ century | Future economics | simulation |

be classified into three groups depending on a time period and study method (Table 6.1).

### 6.2.1 Three Classifications of Economics

The first stage of economics lies approximately in the 1760s to the 1860s. During this century, economics was established as independent science by the time of Quesnay and Smith, and classical economics was established and developed. This age is also referred to as the classical age of economics. The major study method in this age was the literary description.

The second stage of economics begun in the 1870s and has continued until the present. Economics of this age is called neoclassical economics. Such maverick economists as Veblen and Keynes existed during the process of this stage; however, the equilibrium theory was the mainstream in this age. The equilibrium theory has produced various theories setting demand and supply equilibrium and optimal behavior of an agent as a basic framework.

The major study method of economics in this age is the use of mathematics. The use of mathematics had produced the extreme precision of theories that were not observed in the first stage; however, it is based on the assumption that optimization is valid and all things are adjustable at once. If such an assumption can not be established, the neoclassical economic theory becomes unrealistic in fact.

The third stage of economics began the 1980s at earliest, or since the 1990s at the latest. This stage has a common attitude of the previous stages that is to confirm the limitations of mathematical method and try to approach economic phenomena from new viewpoints. However, the third stage does not have any organized frameworks other than that. Based on the complexity concept that focuses on the limitations of mathematical method to approach complicated phenomena, the third stage of economics is no more than forming a part of research programs common to fields of science that approaches complicated phenomena, by making full use of computer technologies. Nevertheless, there are great expectations in the third stage economics because neoclassical economics clearly reaches a deadlock, and a new exit is strongly desired.

### 6.2.2 Deadlock of Neoclassical Economics

The second stage of economics that is represented by the neoclassical economic theory has already faced its limitations. Given that mathematics was the major study method of economics in this stage; such phenomena which mathematics can hardly handle were removed from the analysis as objects. On the other hand, what is suitable for mathematical analysis has been attempted in detail and in large quantities.

The second stage of economics focuses its energy on mathematical refinement having no relation with the reality and problem-solving on details lacking the whole picture. The problems at this stage's of economics have already been introduced over and over, so only the main point is shown here.[1]

The fundamental framework of neoclassical economics is based on the economic views that supply and demand is established for each product setting the price as an independent parameter. The supply and demand functions of neoclassical economics are not a time series that can be observed having time as a parameter. The framework stands on the assumption that supply and demand can be specified to various imaginary prices at a certain point in time. To constitute the supply and demand functions based on the above concept, neoclassical economics formulates consumers' behavior as the 'maximization of utility function indexes under a budget constraint,' and it presumes that producers are faced with diminishing returns (a condition that the average cost per unit increases as production volume increases). Neoclassical economics describes this as a condition that idealizes the realistic; however, it is not only unrealistic but also even anti-realistic. Actually, consumers are following the satisfaction principle that differs from maximization, and in many cases, producers have their own production techniques to increase returns if the returns are not constant.

Neoclassical economics stands on the assumption that the economy reaches a state of equilibrium sooner or later. In the state of equilibrium, people are satisfied with their own behavior and parameters stay constant. This state is a fictitious one, and it will never be reached in the real world. In fact, the concept of equilibrium has become what we call a cognitive obstruction which imposes an incorrect framework on how people behave in the real world and adjust their behavior.

These things have been well indicated over 30 years. Despite this, there is a reason why neoclassical economics is unable to correct these above mentioned theoretical assumptions. If neoclassical economics tries to correct them, it must abandon the framework that the price and trading volume are established by the intersection of demand function with supply function. This is none other than denying the theory of neoclassical economics itself from its foundation. Hence, no matter how these assumptions contradict reality, it is impossible to replace them.

[1] Yoshinori Shiozawa: *A Guide to Economics of Complex System (in Japanese)*, Chap.3, Seisansei Shuppan, 1996.

### *6.2.3 Necessity of a Scientific Revolution in Economics*

Neoclassical economics keeps on maintaining anti-realistic assumptions such as diminishing returns because it is required for a theoretical necessity. By doing so, neoclassical economics accumulates anomalies as a doctrine. This fact clarifies the deadlock of neoclassical economics; in addition, it shows that it is necessary to reform the economic theoretical framework from its very foundation. If using the phrase of Thomas Kuhn here, the second stage economics needs a scientific revolution.

His book *The Structure of Scientific Revolutions* was read also by many economists. The book had a facet to be read that explained the conversion from first stage classical economics to second stage neoclassical economics. In general, however, there was a tacit understanding for an 'economic crises at that time, and many economists admitted the necessity of a scientific revolution in economics.

Such criticisms were actively claimed in the early 1970s. Afterward, however, the rational expectation theory and monetarism became conspicuous, furthermore, the micro-explanation of macroscopic economics had been developed and the game theory has been reorganized. With that, recent young economic researchers take economic crisis as if it had not existed. Those researchers are very busy working out toy problems, and thus escape from working on substantial problems. However, the state of the art never changes by escaping from these problems. Just like the end-stage of geocentric theory, second stage economics has been finely elaborated, while it has an ill-founded theoretical framework. The second stage economics has already come close to the end of paradigm.

## 6.3 New Paradigm and New Study Approach

The concepts of new economics as an alternative to neoclassical economics have been proposed in a wide variety of ways. Economics of complex system or evolutionary economics is one of the concepts. Those economics concepts, however, are regarded as peripheral concepts, not the mainstream of economics. This is because such concepts do not have any alternative analytical tools as strong as methods like mathematics.

The simulation by a multi-agent model or multi-subject model is the result of an effort to make a breakthrough on such circumstances in economics. When such an effort is connected with the reconstitution of economic theory, the second scientific revolution will come to be achieved. What is required now is the introduction of new paradigm, the theory what realizes the new paradigm, and the development of analysis equipment. The third stage of economics cannot be realized by a mere theoretical revolution. It can come to exist only by developing new research tools.

### 6.3.1 Financial Market

Usually, the financial market is believed to be a nearly-complete market. Walras, who created the first framework of neoclassical general equilibrium theory, assumes Paris Bourse as his typical representative of the market. Undoubtedly, the stock exchange can be viewed as the most organized market and a typical form.[2]

However, the idea that the financial market comes close to equilibrium through transaction processes is no more than fiction. In fact, it is almost impossible to deem the market price of a security market as having approached a certain fixed level. For example, Fig. 6.1 shows The Nikkei Average plotted every time the CNBC broadcasting releases this Average; however, nothing indicates a tendency that the price converges on a certain index. Things do not change if research is conducted for a longer term. Fig. 6.2 plots the closing price of The Nikkei Average for 500 days. Here also, the price continuously fluctuates rather than coming close to a constant value. Moreover, the plot shows a certain degree of self-similarity indicating that price fluctuations obey a certain law of movement which generates fractal structure.

The assumption that the price of financial markets or price indexes approaches a certain equilibrium value shows that the second stage economics is restricted by its own framework. As a general analytic framework, the second stage economics can position the economy in the process which changes in terms of time (e.g. period analysis). However, in a more specific analysis, it is usually the case that analysis is conducted with the prices or price indexes having a constant value. It was ever so difficult to analyze the process of continuous fluctuation of prices.[3] If there is any

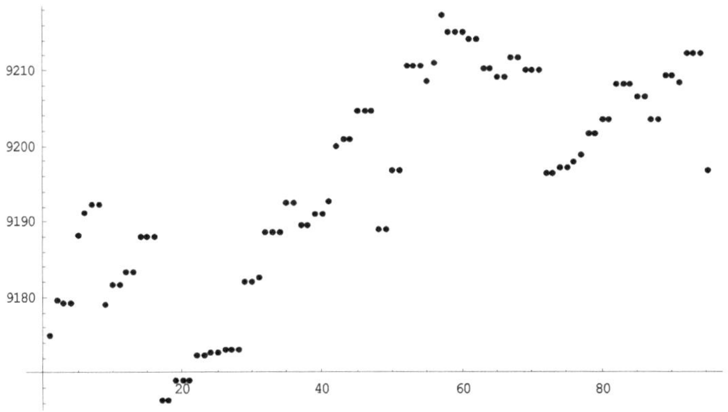


**Fig. 6.1** The Nikkei Average (Morning session 10:00 – 11:00, Sep 5, 2005)

[2] The securities market mainly deals with prices to adjust supply and demand. On the other hand, there are many markets that adjust transaction volumes with constant prices, and such markets have broad ranges. However, there is no doubt that the stock exchange is a typical form of price-adjustment market.

[3] Financial engineering deems the price as a probability process. The advanced mathematical theory, which is the stochastic differential equation, is required to formulate the probability pro-

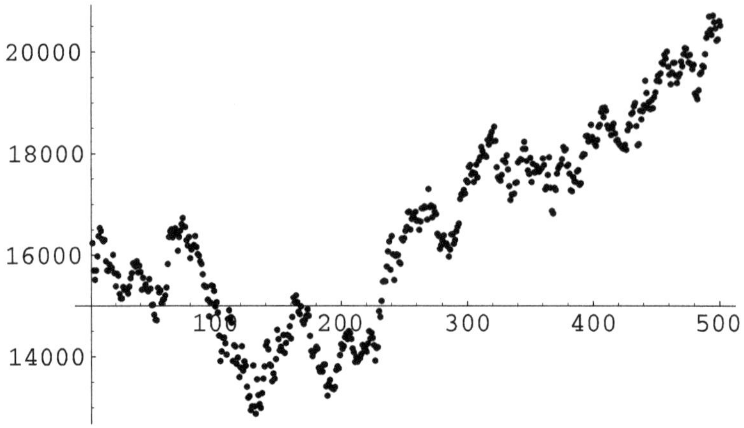


**Fig. 6.2** The Nikkei Average (Daily average, 500 days)

knowledge to be learned under the assumption of equilibrium, it must be allowed as our primary attempt to learn what it is. However, if the equilibrium assumption is set in order to make mathematical analysis available, it would be nothing more than putting the cart before the horse.

If trying to duplicate what is close to the real market process, agent's behavior and also the market obtained as interactions of behavior should be formulated totally as two different things. The first step is putting behavior in the passage of time. With that, a completely different scene from what the equilibrium theory shows will be appeared.

## *6.3.2 Day Traders as an Example*

Let us consider day traders in the market as a specific example. Such traders have come to exist by the substantial lowering of transaction commissions due to the Internet. Many of day traders have a policy that they complete buying and selling within a day and take their positions (offset balance of buying and selling) zero at the end of the day. Regarding ordering, what they refer to is the market price (or price index) movements itself, in addition to news that bursts in sometimes.

For example, when the market opens, a trader places the same amount of buy and sell orders. In this case, the former price is 1 percent higher than the opening price and the latter price is 1 percent lower than the same price. Then he does not care whether the absolute price level goes higher or lower. What he expects is that

---

cess. Financial engineering has a concept which is beyond the second stage economics because it denies the point that a price has a certain convergent value.

the price moves 1% or more up and down. If both orders buying and selling can be contracted before the market closes, this trader is able to have a 2%-margin of profit. If buying and selling commissions are 1% in a round-trip trade, his profit becomes 1%. Day traders assume that a market prices move continuously, and they place buy and sell orders expecting such price movements. In other words, day traders expect that the market does not come to equilibrium; this is exactly the prior condition of investment that these day traders assume.[4]

Such day traders' behavior is not very special in the financial market. In the commodity market, many of traders act assuming such price movements. At least a part of the market participants do not place buy and sell orders corresponding to price level (absolute value of the price itself) as the traditional equilibrium theory assumes, rather, they act based on price movement patterns or the prediction of changes in prices.

The stronger version of equilibrium theory that explains the price becomes constant cannot be utilized for the study of financial market. Under the condition of constant price, day traders cannot exist. The framework using the probability process theory that has been attempted in the field of financial engineering can also not be said to be the best. This framework, basically, assumes that there is no arbitrage opportunity. This is also nothing more than rejecting many traders.

The multi-agent model based simulation does not adopt the approach that configures an analyzable framework first to conduct analysis within its framework. The multi-agent model based simulation observes how the price moves, by constituting almost the identical system with the price formation in the real market. In this sense, the multi-agent model based simulation can be regarded closer as an experiment than a theory. Actually, the expression 'experiment' is often used in U-Mart. It is an experiment conducted in a virtual market, not an experiment conducted in the real market. However, if good model design and well made experimental plan are included in the experiment, it is possible to obtain a lot of information that cannot be obtained in the real market, and gain new knowledge.

### *6.3.3 Possibility of Multi-agent Model*

The characteristics of multi-agent model based simulation can be found in the freeness of agents' behavior specification and diversities. Considering that the real economy is full of diversities, these diversities should be accepted first, and then the way that leads to general knowledge can be taken.

There has been little discussion as to the need for taking into account the variety of behavior in the economy and its changeability. It is not because the fact has not been observed. Although there have been various cases of such observation, if there is no path to take such observations into the theory, the theory has no other choice

[4] Market administrators notice this fact already. They consider that the proper price movements are desirable in order to increase orders to the market.

than to disregard the situation. However, this is a significant problem for economics, considering that diversity is the exact foundation that can establish a market.

The agent-base framework frees economic analysis from the above mentioned stalemate of economics. In the multi-agent model, behavior of each economic agent is realized in the form of a computer program. The computer program specifies the conversion that changes input into output; however, it has an infinite number of possibilities in specifying what to input or output, and specifying the conversion itself. Computing of the program is sequential, so there are no difficulties in making things process on time. Classic mathematical analysis could only handle equilibrium conditions at the most on a stationary process. In the computer calculation, it is easy or rather necessary to formulate behavior of each agent as what is an event driven form.

The freedom in computer calculation allows configuring a variety of settings regarding the interactions among agents. Since financial engineering utilizes the probability theory, usually, it assumes that behavior of each agent is conducted independently. However, no such assumption that implies each behavior or event is an independent phenomenon is needed to trace the changes in a certain situation by using the computer calculation. Here, for example, it is possible to build a mutual dependent relationship into the calculation, which refers to another's decision for self decision.

The expansion of the methods of analysis also expands the theme of analysis. The development of new analytic tools changes not only the theoretical framework of economics but also the theme of economics. As one example, the next section introduces micro-macro loop between behavior and a market.

## 6.4 Behavioral Evolution and Micro-Macro Loop

The formulation of new entity type is realized as a (part of a) computer program. Under this assumption, it is referred to as an agent since it indicates behavior of a certain economic entity. In object programming terminology, this is equivalent to creating a class. This class has agent input and output variables, fields that indicate internal variables and methods that act on such fields. The main method of this class takes in a certain field index as an input, and converts it into an output. The theory regarding the prediction or world of a certain situation that the agent holds is included in the following points: what field should be focused on, what is set as an output, and based on what kind of regulation the input should be set as an output.

### *6.4.1 Behavior Formulation*

Agent's behavior can be complicated depending on the program assembly; however, its fundamental form can be viewed as the CD transformation (from the terms of Tamito Yoshida).

The CD transformation is a conversion that sets a directive order (Directive meaning) configured preliminarily when the result of observing a certain particular external variable is categorized into a certain pattern (Cognitive meaning). The behavioral characteristic of an agent is determined depending on what kind of CD transformation group is held. Behavior is a functional response from the set of C's of cognitive meaning to the set of D's of directive order. The difference of behavior defines individual characteristics of agents.

According to the mathematical computation theory, all kinds of programs can be described as a set of successive implementation of quadruples that are expressed by $qSS'q'$. Here, $q$ and $q'$ express the internal states, $S$ expresses the external state observed, and $S'$ expresses the output toward external. In the case of idealized Turing machine, $S$ expresses a loaded sign that was written on a tape, and $S'$ expresses the right-and-left movements of the tape or writing a certain sign on the tape. The concept of CD transformation does not have any clear reference on how the internal state is regulated. However, since the behavioral entity of humans has memories usually, there is no problem in considering that the behavioral entity contains internal variables. Viewed in this light, the CD transformation has the identical universality with the arbitrage behavioral program.

The classifier system proposed by John Holland is also based on the similar concept. In the classifier system, environment is monitored by a certain bit string, and the bit string is transformed as an output. If the details on classification of bit string are disregarded, this is nothing less than the CD transformation.

By formulating behavior as mentioned above, the process of evolution can be introduced in the computer calculation. It is referred to as Genetic Algorithm (GA) or evolutionary calculation. Introducing the internal condition allows the agent to have memories and the learning function. With that, the agent becomes not mere automatic machine but the existence that can learn and evolve.

### *6.4.2 Micro-Macro Loop*

In a well-organized market like the stock market, various variables can be divided into two layers, micro and macro layers. Micro variables are under the direct control of agents. In the stock market, these variables are equivalent to buy or sell orders of individual agents. Macro variables are commonly recognized by those who participate in the market independent of individual agents. In the case of stock market, these variables indicate stock prices or turnovers.

Where variables can be divided into micro and macro layers and where the inputs of individual agents are limited in what to observe the number of macro variables, a situation can be considered as a typical micro and macro relationship. U-Mart as the theme of this book also has this kind of typical structure. Here, J30 is an exogenous macro variable, the time series and turnover with the futures market price that is determined inside U-Mart are the micro variables. The buying and selling orders placed by individual agents are the micro variables.

There is a double causal relationship between various micro variables and macro variables. If focusing on a certain agent, his input is defined from (the time series of) macro variables and his output is obtained from agent's behavioral rules as a response for the input. In the multi-agent model, the condition is structured in a bottom-up fashion as long as fundamental agent's behavior remains unchanged. With only this reason, the multi-agent model stands on the methodological individualism.

However, the methodological individualism is not a necessary concept for the agent-based simulation. When the evolution of learning or behavior is built into the simulation, the state of macro variables determines which of the micro behaviors of agents are selected.

Such a relationship can be easily understood by using an example. Let us get back to the example of the day trader mentioned in the subsection 6.3.2. The trader was to place the same amount of buy and sell orders with the buying price 1% lower and the selling price 1% higher than the opening price. Let us call this action the strategy *S*. The expected return of the investment strategy *S* depends on how much of fluctuation band the stock price has in one day. There is no loss where sell orders and buy orders are not contracted. If both orders of buying and selling are contracted together, profits are absolutely gained. When either one of selling or buying order is contracted, the day trader faces the danger of suffering loss. For example, where only the buy order is contracted, loss cut should be conducted in order to make positions zero if the stock price falls off more. In contrast, where only the sell order is contracted, the stock price might move upward. After all, the trader suffers loss when the stock price level gets onto either side rapidly; however, he can surely gain profits when the stock price keeps on moving around the level of opening price. His expected profits averagely depend on the stability and volatility of stock price. If the average level of stock price remains almost constant and the fluctuation band of a day is over 2%, the trader can keep on gaining profits with the strategy *S*.

However, such a condition does not last forever. If it is possible for a trader to keep on gaining profits with the above mentioned way, the trader increases the order volume of the strategy *S*. The other traders notice the increased volume, and then they also start to adopt the same strategy. If such kinds of traders increase, a change occurs in the stock price fluctuation band. The stock price is mostly forced to be within $\pm 1\%$ band of the opening price. As with the first effect, such a day that sell and buy orders are not contracted increases. However, the change goes far beyond that. Although the stock price fluctuation band of a day diminishes generally, it does not mean that the stock price level does not change. The second effect is the possibility that the stock price level changes dramatically due to the unexpected breaking news at an unexpected time. At this moment, the expected return index of investment strategy *S* becomes small, that the possibility of traders' gaining a profit also decreases.[5]

The above mentioned example shows that the average profit of an individual traders' strategy depends on the fluctuation mode of price, and the fluctuation mode of price itself changes if the existence rate of traders who have a certain strategy. The interactive regulation relationship can be observed here between micro and macro levels. This is referred to as micro-macro loop.

Fig. 6.3 shows the changes in one-day fluctuation band (high price – low price) of The Nikkei Average for a decade after 1995. Fig. 6.3 takes the quarterly geometric average of high price rate from low price, and plots the difference from 1 in percentage. According to what the figure shows, the one-day fluctuation band declines having a strong tendency after 2001 when day traders started to increase rapidly. Various causes can be considered, and there is the possibility that the above indicates feature works. This is not the experimental result using the multi-agent model; however, this suggests the possibility that the phenomenon, which had been viewed only as a change of external situation by the traditional study method, can be studied under the framework of a multi-agent model.

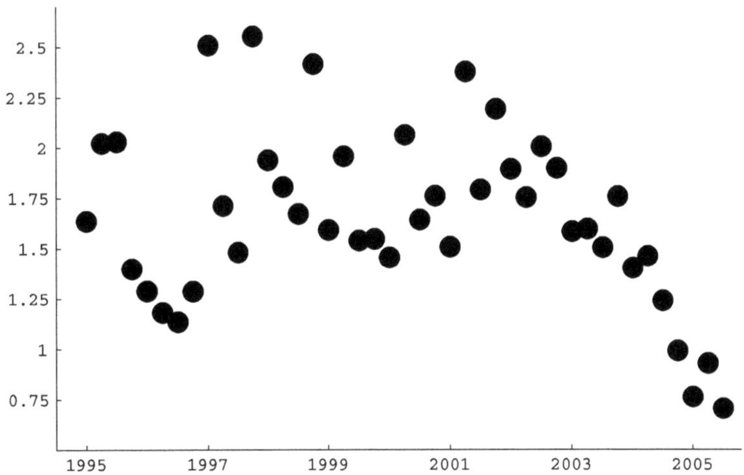


**Fig. 6.3** One-day fluctuation band of the Nikkei Average (average of plotted every three months)

[5] The increase of strategy S makes it easier to cause big and abrupt fluctuations occasionally, in addition to diminishing the daily volatility. This makes the fluctuation distribution have higher peak and wider base than what is traditional.

### 6.4.3 Beyond Methodological Individualism

The reason why micro-macro loop is important is that this situation can become clear evidence against the methodological individualism which lies at the foundation of second stage economics.

Behavior of traders or agents is decided at a certain point in time, and the macro price fluctuation is derived as a result of its own interactions. However, where there is an evolution of behavior on learning, suitable behavior that is selected and adopted also depending on the mode of the macro variables fluctuation. The kind of behavior is what has currently been adopted as a result of the historical selection process. In the event that the behavioral strategy does not change, the whole picture can be structured by an individual agents' behavior. Constructionism based on methodological individualism can be applied to only this aspect. The existence of the micro-macro loop implies that the behavioral rule itself is the result of selection process that depends on the macro fluctuations. Hence, from the viewpoint of micro-macro loop, not only individual behaviors, but also the stability and changeability of macro variables, should be put in question.[6]

In the above consideration of the day trader example, as long as the average expected return has a certain positive value, the percentage of the traders who adopt the strategy $S$ must be increased. However, this process is also self destructive. When the strategy $S$ is widely adopted, the stock price fluctuation mode changes, and the average expected return of the strategy must become small. The efficient market hypothesis claims that such a strategy cannot exist as it promises a positive return rate (above the average). If such a strategy become known and widely used, although it is certain that the strategy will rapidly become self-destructive, it is not always the case that the expected return is always 0. There is the possibility that such a strategy may have a positive expected return temporarily. The action of arbitrage is one thing and the realization of non-arbitrage condition as a result of arbitrage action is another. The strategy having a positive expected return expands as it assemblies over a certain time period, and this eventually leads the strategy to enter into the self-destructive process. Such a process itself should also be viewed as an economic reality. Non-arbitrage condition can be assumed in a priority way.

Technical analysis is a strategy that invests focusing on only the time series of prices or turnovers that was realized in the past. This kind of investment method has been attempted in Japan since the Edo era as a form of chart analysis (called *Keisen*). When a certain analysis or an investment strategy was discovered, a positive return could have been expected from that analysis. However, after going through the above mentioned process, the expected returns of the analysis must have come close to almost 0. However, this fact does not imply that all the profit-earning opportunities are already discovered.

Economy does have such a history. In agent-based modeling, such a history can also be examined. Theoretical economics has excluded a history for a long time

[6] This is described more precisely in my "About Micro-Macro Loop," *Economics Review* (Kyoto University, Japanese series), volume 164, No. 5, pp. 1 – 73, Oct, 2000.

since the second stage economics allows only a simple model design. In the second stage economics there was no room for the history.

## 6.5 Review and Perspective of U-Mart Project

This chapter has handled the possibility of a multi-agent model based simulation. However, this is nothing more than a possibility. Not all of the agent based models lead to or develop the third stage of economics. Sadly, in multi-agent based models, there are many models in which agent behavior has not been properly formulized, or the interactions among agents do not express economic transactions well. Even in the models that are regarded as pioneers in this field, such as Axelrod, many of such models are still in the figurative phase.

### *6.5.1 U-Mart as Artificial Market*

Recently, however, two outstanding results have been achieved in Japan. One is the "Artificial Market" model developed by the group of Dr. Kiyoshi Izumi.[7] This model aims at simulating the Yen-Dollar exchange market, and is an example on the level that should become the future standard in view of model building, as well as the result obtained by the model simulation. In the model's architecture, 17 kinds of time series are converted to data as environmental variables for the model, such as economic indicator, price index, short-term interest rate, and total money supply. Interviews were also conducted with exchange dealers. With regard to their behavior at a certain point in time, the interviews asked on what kind of judgment was such behavior based, and then the interview results were reflected in the agents' behavioral rules. Additionally, regarding the simulation results, this model has achieved remarkable accomplishments, such as succeeding in the reemergence (recreation) of the bubble economy. Approximately three-quarters of the simulations conducted showed a bubble and the outburst of the bubble during the time period in which we actually observed a bubble in the real economy.

The other is U-Mart introduced in this book. U-Mart is not a pure agent-based model, but as already introduced, it is a market simulation in which human agents (humans) can participate together with machine agents. U-Mart can be used either experiment, an experiment with only human agents or only with machine agents. However, the U-Mart feature, that allows human and machine agents can participate in transactions simultaneously and the results can be compared, makes U-Mart's grounding in the reality very special.

For example, the following observations and analyses can be conducted.

[7] Kiyoshi Izumi: *Artificial Market / Complex Approach for Market Analysis* (in Japanese), Morikita Shuppan, 2003.

(1) By observing human agents, including psychological aspects, behavior shown by the actual traders can be examined.
(2) By comparing experiments only by human agents with the experiments only by machine agents, the effect of machine agents and behavioral effectiveness can be examined.
(3) If no significant difference is observed between the market in which only machine agents participate and in which only human agents participate, the market formed by only the machine agents can be examined as a reasonable model of the real market. An experiment only by machine agents can then be conducted at high speed. This allows for a mass amount of experiments that change conditions in diverse ways to be conducted in short periods of time.

These things have been already attempted and can be viewed as an excellent characteristic of U-Mart. Since participants can experience the transaction experiment in almost the same condition as an actual market, U-Mart can be utilized as good study material that serves to greater understanding futures market.[8]

U-Mart contributes to research as the support means. Vernon Smith and Daniel Kahneman, who were awarded the Nobel Prize for Economics in 2002, have drawn much attention to the fields of experimental economics and behavioral economics. Those economics discovered various distortions of economic behavior that are impossible to explain with only rationality, and anomaly in financial markets. However, both behavioral economics and experimental economics are restricted within the possible setting of experimental environments. In many cases, the condition settings depend on a verbal explanation. On the other hand, U-Mart has an advantage that it can provide an experimental environment having appropriate complexity. U-Mart can be an important tool in order to clarify the universal issue that explains decision making in a certain complicated situation.[9]

From the initial stage of the project, U-Mart aims at providing a test-bed for market research as one of its purposes. Hence, the U-Mart group welcomes that the U-Mart system be utilized in experiments and education by the hands of those researchers who are not the original developers. Introductory lectures for researchers have already been held on many occasions so far, and the publication of this book is an additional part of such activities.

### *6.5.2 Some Methodological Issues*

A considerable number of experiments have been conducted in many universities since U-Mart actually began to be utilized. Yet, there still remain many experimental themes that should be attempted and developed in the future. U-Mart seems to be headed in the direction that an experimental plan can be designed having more

[8] As described in the preface, U-Mart is effectively utilized in computer technology education.

[9] Research in this direction has been attempted in Hakodate Mirai University.

limited purpose, over an above the phase of actual operation and the enjoyment of participation.

In this regard, however, since the experiment using U-Mart is not merely conducted under a complicated environment, it differs from those experiments in the past in quality, because the experiment includes various methodological issues in analysis and interpretation of experimental results or experimental planning itself, which have not been regarded as problems in past research.

A multi-agent model study generally proceeds in a series of phases. This is not only applicable to U-Mart. The following shows the main flow.

(1) Observation and examination of the target system
(2) (Re-) Formation of the agent-based model
(3) Simulations using the model
(4) Analysis of the simulation results, and comparison with the target system
(5) Examination of the model validity itself
(6) Obtaining knowledge and discovery from research

These phases are not necessarily time series that are linearly processed. As mentioned in the scene of research management development, these phases are concurrent ones. Especially, since regression often required from phase (5) to (1) or (2). Through this series of studies, it is possible to achieve phase (6) i.e., knowledge which cannot be obtained by any other research method. This is the aim of the multi-agent based model research program.

This does not only apply to multi-agent based models. In general there is the criticism of computer based experiments, which says that researchers can only obtain findings by using a test-and-see style method, in other words, "when we try this, this is what happens." As a model becomes more complex, the greater variety of results can be obtained. Just because the same movements with the target system were obtained does not mean that the model validity is ensured. In a complex system, it is also possible to have the view that almost any results can be produced. From this perspective, the only fact is that the result desired and obtained are inadequate.

What is required for the knowledge that is obtained by simulation or experiments to be trustworthy? It would be a falsehood if someone stated that the review of these kinds of issues is progressing.

As far as phase (4) is concerned, the following problem can be cited. If the target system and model are complex systems, it is impossible to expect whether the time series of corresponding variables traces the same path. In terms of philosophy, the time series observed and the time series generated by simulation, they belong each to a different possible world. When having these time series that belong to different worlds, the model system should reconstruct the mechanism of target system. Under such a circumstance, how can we examine whether the analysis of a model can provide knowledge regarding what the real world should be?

Although it is impossible to check raw data, there is a case that a certain abstraction allows data to be checked. For example, if it is impossible to expect that two time series of a price accord with each other, then we can examine the fluctuation distribution to confirm whether they are the same type. The artificial market constructed by the group of Dr. Izumi has shown that the fluctuation of exchange rates became the distribution actually observed that is closer than the random walk distribution (in other words, the distribution that has the higher peak and wider tail than the lognormal distribution).

In such verification, there is a possibility that the quality assigned by the experimental environment setting is being picked up. For example, U-Mart provides the stock price index from outside as a part of experimental environment. Since the stock price index and index futures price diverge, so that in a short term, their fluctuation distribution can be different. There is much point in studying the distribution characteristics of index futures price fluctuation. In a mid-and-long term with the case of U-Mart, however, the futures price follows the stock price index.[10] For example, if the Hurst exponent is measured to observe the long-term fluctuation characteristics of price and what is very close to the result of actual market is obtained, it duplicates the fluctuation characteristics merely, which were configured as the experimental environment.

That is not to say that there is a way to distinguish the meaning of experimental results automatically. For quite a while, there is no way except correcting many errors by using various trial-and-error methods. Centuries of experiences have been required to establish an experimental method, which is essential for modern science. Computer simulation including U-Mart is what should be called the third scientific study approach after the theory and experiment. We must realize that we are still standing on the threshold of that approach.

Phase (5), which examines the model's validity, faces more difficult problems. In this phase, grounding in reality must be attempted from various viewpoints. It is impossible to expect that this problem will be deepened with general and abstract discussion. This problem should continuously be reexamined with view to promote the specific research program such as U-Mart project. The U-Mart project also requires such a challenge towards methodological issues.

### *6.5.3 Success Factors of U-Mart*

Although facing many issues, undoubtedly, U-Mart has achieved a fair degree of success. U-Mart builds an important milestone on the huge objective of trying to develop a new study tool for economics taking advantage of computer technologies. However, the development of a new study tools should be continued from many different approaches. As a hint for such a challenge, let us look back on the simply reasons why U-Mart could achieve success. It could be a hint to serve to organize research that integrates the humanities and science, which has recently been proposed.

---

[10] In the actual market, the index futures price moves the stock price index because of arbitration.

There are many difficulties in promoting the research program known as the simulation by multi-agent models. A program design and implementation on such a broad scale as U-Mart cannot be realized without proactive participation of information engineering experts. The most important factor in U-Mart success can be found in a positive cooperative relationship which is developed between engineers and economists.

This cooperative relationship was dependent on many coincidences. It all started with Emergent Symposium of The Society of Instruments and Control Engineers. During the symposium gathering the same evening, the author discussed the possibility of an interesting and untapped study subject in economics, and the cooperation of engineers could make it possible. It was nothing short of a miracle that people appeared who offered cooperation on this project. In November 6, 1998, Hajime Kita, Hiroshi Deguchi, and Yoshinori Shiozawa discussed the project outline during a meeting at New Otani Hotel in Akasaka, Tokyo. No specific research expenses were assigned at that time; however, thanks to Prof. Takao Terano, a study group was formed with those who were interested in the project at Otsuka school campus of Tsukuba University.

In the subsequent process, the main leader changed on a case-by-case basis. There is no page for looking back at the process; however, Hajime Kita has indicated what was needed to maintain the cooperative relationship, which is described as follows. When the experts in several fields work together, the relationship must not take a form that one is dependent on another, or one uses another. He indicated that collaborative research cannot be continued without some merit for all researchers of different study fields. In the case of U-Mart, it is a matter of course that economists can easily utilize the findings of the U-Mart project. For those engineers who spent a lot of time on the work on implementing U-Mart, what kind of meaning could they have through participating in the U-Mart project? One positive achievement of the U-Mart project was that each respective engineer could utilize the completed system in accord with their interests, such as study materials for inverse problems or project based education. The project goal was to build a common test-bed which could be used even in an unexpected ways.

The second factor is a reasonably good degree of system design. A multi-agent model for social science study assumes to be complicated to some degree and be a broad scale system. Such freedom is the possibility of multi-agent model; however, the following things are required to realize such a complicated and broad scale system: large-scale data acquisition, system design, and data entry works. One of the many positives of U-Mart is that it has a part of reflecting the environmental complexity which is confined to one of the stock price index series. A vast amount of actual data is available in this regard. It also makes possible to generate virtual data.[11] Upon conducting an experiment, such data can be replaced. Although the time series of stock price index has a simple structure, it realizes the situational complexity that can provide adequate stimulus for participants.

[11] This is also one of the interesting themes related to U-Mart.

With regard to model building, there is the strong temptation to internalize more factors. However, if trying to incorporate various factors or interactions into a model, such an attempt could heavily burden situation-building inside the model. The situational settings should not be complicated without reason, except where the achievement is in accordance with the effort made can be expected. In U-Mart, at least at the present time, the judgment of investors is limited into using technical analysis. It is not difficult to formulate a vision for including fundamental analysis in the investors' judgments. However, can it be possible to achieve such results compatible with the burdens required for such an expansions?

The multi-agent model can be built on almost any field of study. However, that is not to say that there are clear conditions for simulation by multi-agent models to be a good study tool. Design and selection of the basic model structure should be based on sophisticated decisions; however, the knowledge that draws such decisions is excursive and unclear. The U-Mart success significantly depended on coincidences, and we cannot deny the fact that its success significantly depended on selecting of an area where the market which determines the futures price had a given stock price index.

## 6.6 Future Issues and Perspective

With an excellent graphic user interface (GUI), U-Mart is currently has a stable system that is also available for those non-experts. The system source code was released to public previously, and we hope that more people will be lead to utilize the U-Mart system with the publication of this book. There is no doubt that one important stage has been finished. However, it does not imply that the U-Mart project comes to an end. Utilizing the current accomplishments of the system, the U-Mart project group or other independent researchers and project groups can develop their own respective study themes.

Let us now touch one of such activities, which is the research theme that we are working on. It is research on a thin market. This is absolutely an example of the future issues. U-Mart is a common test-bed, and its use is not limited only to development groups. We desire that novel study themes can be produced and pursued, beyond the compass of our current imagination.

### *6.6.1 Thin Market*

When talking about a market and price in economics, the market that has already been established is implied. In reality, however, it is not easy to manage an organized market. Such a market can never be run without having enough transaction fees to cover all the costs necessary for the market management. The price cannot be fixed in such a way as supposed in the neoclassical economics, if the number of orders is small. If you observe the market conditions column of Osaka Securities Exchange, many of the stock brands are listed as "quote prices" indicating that transactions are not contracted. This is because there are many stock brands that go on the market that overlap with the ones in Tokyo Stock Exchange. This is a good example to show that there are markets where the transactions are not easily contracted.

The problem is that there is an unseen market, currently a nonexistent market. There are many countries in the world and the size of each country's economy varies. The reality is that countries such a Japan with large scale economies are very few. Many countries cannot organize a securities exchange even it is necessity. Except for securities, there are various products that are unsuitable for a bilateral negotiation. The losses derived from the nonexistence of these markets are unseen; however, it should be mentioned that this does not mean that the price of loss is insignificant.

A market, where it is difficult to make a contract or having a small number of orders during a certain period, is referred to as a market with thin board, or simply, a thin market. The thin market has a structural paradox. The expense per one order costs high due to the small number of orders. When making transaction fees to cover the expenses, the rate of exchange fees will be higher. Commodity liquidity is low due to the difficulty in pricing. Holdings for speculation and investment purposes are avoided. As a result, the number of buy and sell orders decreases. The price is very difficult to be determined. The possibility is great that such a thin market will fall into a negative spiral.

The question then arises. Is it possible to reverse such negative spirals? If market liquidity can be increased with low costs, then the market placed near to the threshold can be managed. Such measures have been already attempted in many markets. However, this fact has barely been considered from the field of economics. The reason easily can be estimated. It is because economics has never had the means, methods, or the theories required for studying such markets.

Can this so called vacuum be filled using the U-Mart system? From this standpoint, the theme "thin market study" was selected. Using the U-Mart system, this theme was highlighted as a result of the search for study issues that cannot be realized by other study methods.

This study project has just been launched, and two directional properties are being examined.

One direction is research on the thin market itself. In this research, at first, the thin market is actually created to observe transactions. U-Mart makes it possible to realize this. This was done by only removing the random agents introduced to increase the contract rate. The comparison between the *Itayose* (board making) market and continuous auction market is cited as the target of second stage research. It was impossible to simulate the continuous auction market with the original U-Mart system. Now a new version of the system has been implemented after necessary changes were made to the market specification, so that a continuous auction market experiment can be conducted.[12]

[12] As the study progresses, such changes are often required. Although this must be burden to programmers, they accept this opportunity as an experience of an agile programming.

The other direction is a market design that improves the speed of pricing to increase the contract rate under conditions where an increased order frequency and an increased number of orders can not be realized. This direction must be realized if the role of the market maker is to be described as a computer program.

As a matter of course, there is a problem. Can a computerized market maker be made strong enough to handle malicious traders? Market makers do not have to gain profits; however, they must not make losses. This stability must be guaranteed, under the restriction that the orders placed in the market are accepted in principle. Here, many of the practical and theoretical problems are involved. From the viewpoint of computational theory, such a program might be impossible to be created. Although it is impossible to create such a program in principle, there might be a level at which the program could become a practical reality. The only way to resolve this issue is through examination on an experimental basis under various conditions. Study of this nature could not be possible without the environment provided by U-Mart.

### *6.6.2 Support for Institutional Design*

The thin market study makes it possible to realize a transaction market under a particular condition. This is a study that creates something out of nothing; however, U-Mart can also serve to a study of markets that exist actually.

In a high-level market such as a securities market, a variety of institutions are adopted according to circumstances. The market micro structures are extremely varied, such as the *Itayose* and *Zaraba* (continuous auction market), the role of market makers, the availability of book order information, price movement limit, and circuit breakers. These respective institutions have been considered in accord with each occasion; however, their functions and effects are not always clear. Such study has been hampered because of the universal reason that it is difficult to conduct experiments under the identical conditions. U-Mart has a possibility to change this situation.

This chapter has focused on how a multi-agent model simulation can contribute to innovation in economics research tools and to what extent such an examination progresses in the U-Mart project. If economics is a science that studies the economy and if research tools are to be innovative, it becomes necessary for these new tools to serve as innovators for economics itself. Conversely, this is only true in such occasions when the research tools innovations can be seen as real. In both the fields of economics and research tool development, the U-Mart project has shown an adequate amount of potential.

# Appendix A
# Attached CD-ROM Composition

- README.pdf: Attached CD-ROM composition, how to use, and additional information
- LICENSE.pdf: The license of U-Mart system
- Doc folder: The folder contains various documents
  - JPN folder
    - explanationOfStrateties folder: The description of 10 types of agents embedded in the U-Mart System by default (Japanese).
    - Tutorial.pdf: The U-Mart System Tutorial File (Japanese).
    - UMartPamphlet.pdf: The U-Mart Project Pamphlet (Japanese).
  - ENG folder
    - explanationOfStrategies folder: The description of 10 types of agents embedded in the U-Mart System by default (English).
    - Tutorial.pdf: The U-Mart System Tutorial File (English).
    - UMartPamphlet.pdf: The U-Mart Project Pamphlet (English).
- UMartSystem-Linux.zip: The U-Mart system for Linux. To use this, unzip the folder after copying the file to HDD.
- UMartSystem-Mac.zip: The U-Mart system for Mac OS X (PowerPC). To use this, unzip the folder after copying the file to HDD. This folder does not contain JRE since Mac OS X has Java environment by default.
- UMartSystem-Windows folder: The U-Mart system for Windoes2000/XP. (Copy each folder to HDD.)
  - LICENSE.pdf: The U-Mart System License
  - Icon folder: Various icons
  - jre folder: JAVA2 Runtime Environment for Windows
  - resources folder: U-Mart System Settings Files
    - csv folder: Settings files
    - images folder: Image files
    - tutorial folder: Help and tutorial files

  - strategy folder: The source files (***.java) and class files (***.class) of the machine agents embedded in the U-Mart system by default
  - MarketSimulator_ja.exe: Stand alone version of Market Simulator for Windows (Japanese)
  - MarketSimulator_en.exe: Stand alone version of Market Simulator for Windows (English)
  - MarketServer_ja.exe: Network version of Market Server for Windows (Japanese)
  - MarketServer_en.exe: Network version of Market Server for Windows (English)
  - TradingTerminal_ja.exe: Network version of Trading Terminal for Windows (Japanese)
  - TradingTerminal_en.exe: Network version of Trading Terminal for Windows (English)
  - LogAnalyzer.exe: Log analyzing program for Windows
  - UMartSystem.jar: U-Mart system JAR file
  - LogAnalyzer.1.3.1.jar: Log Analyzer JAR file

- When unzipping UMartSystem-Linux.zip and UMartSystem-Mac.zip, the 'exe' file turns into 'sh' and 'app' file, respectively. Additionally, UMartSystem-Linux.zip folder contains JAVA2 Runtime Environment for Linux.

# Appendix B
# Log Format

## B.1 Log Format of Market Simulator and Market Server

When logs are created using the Market Simulator and Market Server, the folder "UMARTxxxxxx (the executed date and time on the millisecond time scale are entered in 'xxxxxx' part)" is created in the same hierarchy, and the logs are saved in this folder in the CSV format.

- UMARTxxxxxx
  - Memver.csv: Various settings for the agent participants in the transaction experiment.
  - Price.csv: The time series used in the transaction experiment. Where the futures price has not been determined, it is kept blank instead of the index '-1' entered.
  - Settlement_account.csv: Agents' final transaction results
  - TimeSeriesDefinitions.cev: Settings of the time series and experimental conditions used in the transaction experiment.
  - account: Agents' transaction results
    - Day1Session1_account.csv: The agents' transaction results of the first session on the first day.
    - Day1_MM_account.csv: The agents' transaction results after Mark-to-Market on the first day.
    - Settlement_account.csv: Agents' final transaction results
  - execution: Agents' contract records
    - Day1Session1_execution.csv: The agents' contract records of the first session on the first day.
  - order: Agents' ordering records
    - Day1Session1_order.csv: The agents' ordering records of the first session on the first day.
  - order_book: Order book

- Day1Session1_order_book.csv: The order book of the first session on the first day.

## B.2 Log Format of Trading Terminal

When using the Trading Terminal, logs can be saved with filenames specified after the transaction. The following four csv files are be saved.

- ****_price.csv: The time series used in the transaction experiment. Where the futures price has not been determined, it is kept blank instead of the index '-1' entered.
- ****_order.csv: Ordering records
- ****_position.csv: Position transitions
- ****_profit.csv: Profit transitions

# Appendix C
# Machine Agents Embedded in the U-Mart System

There are 10 types of machine agents that are embedded in the U-Mart system. All source code is contained in the 'Strategy' folder. Hereinafter, each algorithm of the10 types of machine agents and the parameters that can be specified by settings files are introduced.

TrendStrategy

*Algorithm outline*

This agent obtains the futures price (U-Mart price) of previous session and the session before the previous session. If the futures price cannot be obtained, the spot price is used. If both of the prices are unavailable, the constant number (the field variable, 'nominalPrice') is used. This agent places a buy order when the previous session price is higher than the session price before the previous session, and places a sell order when the previous session price is lower than the session price before the previous session. The order price is randomly determined using Gaussian with a focus on the latest price obtained. The divergence of price distribution is determined with the field variable 'widthOfPrice.' The order volume is randomly determined between minQuote and maxQuote.

*Parameters*

| Parameter | Type | Role | Range | Initial value | Meaning | |
|---|---|---|---|---|---|---|
| widthOf Price | int | Dispersion of probability variable to determine the limit price | 1 | ··· | 1000 | 20 |
| maxQuote | int | Maximum order volume per one order | (minQuote+1) … (initial cash/300,000) | 50 | | |
| minQuote | int | Minimum order volume per one order | 1 | ··· | (maxQuote-1) | 10 |
| max Position | int | Maximum value of actual positions, which are used for asset management. | 1 … (initial cash/300,000) | 300 | | |

## AntiTrendStrategy

*Algorithm outline*

This agent obtains the futures price (U-Mart price) of previous session and the session before the previous session. If the futures price cannot be obtained, the spot price is used. If both of prices are unavailable, the constant number (the field variable, 'nominalPrice') is used. This agent places a buy order when the previous session price is lower than the session price before the previous session, and places a sell order when the previous session price is higher than the session price before the previous session. The order price is randomly determined using Gaussian with a focus on the latest price obtained. The divergence of price distribution is determined with the field variable 'widthOfPrice.' The order volume is randomly determined between minQuote and maxQuote.

*Parameters*

| Parameter | Type | Role | Range | Initial value | Meaning | |
|---|---|---|---|---|---|---|
| widthOf Price | int | Dispersion of probability variable to determine the limit price | 1 | ··· | 1000 | 20 |
| maxQuote | int | Maximum order volume per one order | (minQuote+1) ... (initial cash/300,000) | 50 | | |
| minQuote | int | Minimum order volume per one order | 1 | ··· | (maxQuote-1) | 10 |
| max Position | int | Maximum value of actual positions, which are used for asset management. | 1 ... (initial cash/300,000) | 300 | | |

## RandomStrategy

*Algorithm outline*

This agent determines whether to place sell or buy orders in a random manner, and obtains the latest futures price (U-Mart price). The agent uses the spot price if the futures price cannot be obtained. If both of the prices are unavailable, the constant number (the field variable, 'nominalPrice') is used. The order price is randomly determined using Gaussian with a focus on the latest price obtained. The divergence of price distribution is determined with the field variable 'widthOfPrice.' The order volume is randomly determined between minQuote and maxQuote.

*Parameters*

| Parameter | Type | Role | Range | Initial value | Meaning | |
|---|---|---|---|---|---|---|
| widthOf Price | int | Dispersion of probability variable to determine the limit price | 1 | ··· | 1000 | 20 |
| maxQuote | int | Maximum order volume per one order | (minQuote+1) ... (initial cash/300,000) | 50 | | |
| minQuote | int | Minimum order volume per one order | 1 | ··· | (maxQuote-1) | 10 |
| max Position | int | Maximum value of actual positions, which are used for asset management. | 1 ... (initial cash/300,000) | 300 | | |

SRandomStrategy

*Algorithm outline*

This agent determines whether to place sell or buy orders in random manner, and obtains the latest spot price. The agent uses the futures price if the spot price cannot be obtained. If both of prices are unavailable, the contract number (the field variable, 'nominalPrice') is used. The order price is randomly determined using Gaussian with a focus on the latest price obtained. The divergence of price distribution is determined with the field variable 'widthOfPrice.' The order volume is randomly determined between minQuote and maxQuote.

*Parameters*

| Parameter | Type | Role | Range | Initial value | Meaning | | |
|---|---|---|---|---|---|---|---|
| widthOf Price | int | Dispersion of probability variable to determine the limit price | 1 | … | 1000 | 20 | |
| maxQuote | int | Maximum order volume per one order | (minQuote+1) … (initial cash/300,000) | 50 | | | |
| minQuote | int | Minimum order volume per one order | 1 | … | (maxQuote-1) | 10 | |
| max Position | int | Maximum value of actual positions, which are used for asset management. | 1 … (initial cash/300,000) | 300 | | | |
| reference Term | int | Term for calculating the moving average | 4 | … | 20 | 10 | Index seems to be appropriate empirically |
| edgeBand | double | Specifies the RSI edge-band | 0 | … | 1 | 0.3 | Index used in general |

## RsiStrategy

*Algorithm outline*

This agent obtains the futures price (U-Mart price), and uses the spot price if the futures price cannot be obtained. Based on the value obtained, RSI is calculated. RSI = up-Sum / (upSum+downSum). Here, 'upSum' expresses the sum total of price fluctuation when the price rises, and 'downSum' expresses the sum total of price fluctuation when the price falls. This agent places a sell order if the RSI value is higher than the upper limit (1.0-edge band value), and places a buy order if the RSI value is lower than the lower limit (edge band value). The order price is randomly determined using Gaussian with a focus on the latest futures price obtained. The divergence of price distribution is determined with the field variable 'widthOfPrice.' The order volume is randomly determined between minQuote and maxQuote.

*Parameters*

| Parameter | Type | Role | Range | Initial value | Meaning | | |
|---|---|---|---|---|---|---|---|
| widthOf Price | int | Dispersion of probability variable to determine the limit price | 1 | … | 1000 | 20 | |
| maxQuote | int | Maximum order volume per one order | (minQuote+1) … (initial cash/300,000) | 50 | | | |
| minQuote | int | Minimum order volume per one order | 1 | … | (maxQuote-1) | 10 | |
| max Position | int | Maximum value of actual positions, which are used for asset management. | 1 … (initial cash/300,000) | 300 | | | |
| reference Term | int | Term to count the number of price rising or falling | 4 | … | 20 | 10 | Index seems to be appropriate empirically |
| edgeBand | double | Specifies the RSI edge-band | 0 | … | 1 | 0.3 | Index used in general |

## SRsiStrategy

*Algorithm outline*

This agent obtains the spot price, and uses the futures price if the spot price cannot be obtained. Based on the value obtained, RSI is calculated. RSI = upSum / (upSum+downSum). Here, upSum expresses the sum total of price fluctuation when the price rises, and downSum expresses the sum total of price fluctuation when the price falls. This agent places a sell order if the RSI value is higher than the upper limit (1.0-edge band value), and places a buy order if the RSI value is lower than the lower limit (edge band value). The order price is determined using Gaussian with a focus on the latest spot price obtained. The divergence of price distribution is determined with the field variable 'widthOfPrice.' The order volume is randomly determined between minQuote and maxQuote.

*Parameters*

| Parameter | Type | Role | Range | Initial value | Meaning | | |
|---|---|---|---|---|---|---|---|
| widthOf Price | int | Dispersion of probability variable to determine the limit price | 1 | … | 1000 | 20 | |
| maxQuote | int | Maximum order volume per one order | (minQuote+1) … (initial cash/300,000) | 50 | | | |
| minQuote | int | Minimum order volume per one order | 1 | … | (maxQuote-1) | 10 | |
| max Position | int | Maximum value of actual positions, which are used for asset management. | 1 … (initial cash/300,000) | 300 | | | |
| reference Term | int | Term for calculating the moving average | 4 | … | 20 | 10 | Index seems to be appropriate empirically |
| edgeBand | double | Specifies the RSI edge-band | 0 | … | 1 | 0.3 | Index used in general |

## MovingAverageStrategy

*Algorithm outline*

This agent calculates the moving average of futures price between short term and mid term. It checks whether the short-term moving average intersects with the mid-term moving average or not. Orders are placed when they intersect with each other. Checking the trend of short-term moving average, this agent places a buy order when the price rises, and places a sell order when the price falls. Where $Dp$ indicates the difference of absolute value between the previous session futures price and the futures price before the previous session, the limit order is expressed with the following formula:

$$\text{previous session's futures price} + Dp + (Dp / 4) \times \text{Gaussian}$$

The order volume is given by the uniform distribution between minQuote and maxQuote.

*Parameters*

| Parameter | Type | Role | Range | Initial value | Meaning | |
|---|---|---|---|---|---|---|
| maxQuote | int | Maximum order volume per one order | (minQuote+1) … (initial cash/300,000) | 50 | | |
| minQuote | int | Minimum order volume per one order | 1 | … | (maxQuote-1) | 10 |
| max Position | int | Maximum value of actual positions, which are used for asset management. | 1 … (initial cash/300,000) | 300 | | |
| short Reference Term | int | Term for calculating the short-term moving average | 4 | … | medium Reference Term | 10 |
| medium Reference Term | int | Term for calculating the mid-term moving average | shortReference Term | … | 30 | 20 |

SMovingAverageStrategy

*Algorithm outline*

This agent calculates the moving average of spot price between short term and mid term. It checks whether the short-term moving average intersects with the mid-term moving average or not. Orders are placed when they intersect with each other. Checking the trend of short-term moving average, this agent places a buy order when the price rises, and places a sell order when the price falls. Where *Dp* indicates the difference of absolute value between the previous session spot price and the spot price before the previous session, the limit order is expressed with the following formula:

$$\text{previous session's spot price} + Dp + (Dp / 4) \times \text{Gaussian}$$

The order volume is given by the uniform distribution between minQuote and maxQuote.

*Parameters*

| Parameter | Type | Role | Range | Initial value | Meaning | |
|---|---|---|---|---|---|---|
| maxQuote | int | Maximum order volume per one order | (minQuote+1) … (initial cash/300,000) | 50 | | |
| minQuote | int | Minimum order volume per one order | 1 | … | (maxQuote-1) | 10 |
| max Position | int | Maximum value of actual positions, which are used for asset management. | 1 … (initial cash/300,000) | 300 | | |
| short Reference Term | int | Term for calculating the short-term moving average | 4 | … | medium Reference Term | 10 |
| medium Reference Term | int | Term for calculating the mid-term moving average | shortReference Term | … | 30 | 20 |

## SFSpreadStrategy

*Algorithm outline*

This agent obtains the latest futures price (U-Mart price) and spot price. Orders are placed when the interval between the spot price and futures price diverges from the threshold. This agent places a buy order if the futures price is lower than the spot price, and places a sell order if the futures price is higher than the spot price. Where the futures price at $t$-term is $p(t)$ and the probability variable corresponds to $N(1,0)$ is $x$, the order price is determined the following formula:

$$(p(t)+p(t-1))/2+\text{abs}(p(t)-p(t-1))\times x$$

The order volume is determined with the uniform distribution between minQuote and maxQuote.

*Parameters*

| Parameter | Type | Role | Range | Initial value | Meaning | | |
|---|---|---|---|---|---|---|---|
| widthOf Price | int | Dispersion of probability variable to determine the limit price | 1 | ··· | 1000 | 20 | |
| maxQuote | int | Maximum order volume per one order | (minQuote+1) ··· (initial cash/300,000) | 50 | | | |
| minQuote | int | Minimum order volume per one order | 1 | ··· | (maxQuote-1) | 10 | |
| max Position | int | Maximum value of actual positions, which are used for asset management. | 1 ··· (initial cash/300,000) | 300 | | | |
| spread Ratio Threshold | double | Threshold of rate of divergence between futures and spot prices used to judge ordering | 0 | ··· | 1 | 0.001 | Determined empirically. |

## DayTradeStrategy

*Algorithm outline*

This agent obtains the latest futures price (U-Mart price), and uses the spot price if the futures price cannot be obtained. If both of prices are unavailable, the constant number (the field variable, 'nominalPrice') is used. Where the latest futures price is $P$ and spreadRatio is $R$, the limit buy order price is determined with $(1+R)\times P$. Similarly, the limit sell order price is determined with $(1-R)\times P$. The order volume is determined with the uniform random numbers between minQuote and maxQuote.

*Parameters*

| Parameter | Type | Role | Range | Initial value | Meaning | |
|---|---|---|---|---|---|---|
| maxQuote | int | Maximum order volume per one order | (minQuote+1) … (initial cash/300,000) | 50 | | |
| minQuote | int | Minimum order volume per one order | 1 | … | (maxQuote-1) | 10 |
| max Position | int | Maximum value of actual positions, which are used for asset management. | 1 … (initial cash/300,000) | 300 | | |
| short Reference Term | int | Term for calculating the short-term moving average | 4 | … | medium Reference Term | 10 |
| medium Reference Term | int | Term for calculating the mid-term moving average | shortReference Term | … | 30 | 20 |

# Appendix D
# Publication List

Academic Journals

- Rikiya Fukumoto, Hajime Kita: "Mokuteki Identeki Algolithm wo mochita jinkoushijou no tameno torihiki agent no kousei", *Academic journal of Japan Society for Simulation Technology*, 21, 2, 154-161, 2002.
- Kazuhisa Taniguchi: "Human Agent ni yoru U-Mart experiment report", *Osaka Sangyo University Economics*, vol.4, no.2, 85-104, 2003.
- Y.Shiozawa: "Evolutionary Economcis in the 21st Century: A Manifest", *Evolutinary and Institional Economics Review*, 1, 1, pp.5-47, 2004.
- Yoshihiro Nakajima, Hiroyuki Matsui: "U-Mart Project no gaiyou", *Keisoku toseigyo*, 43, 12, 2005.
- H.Kita, K.Tahiguchi, I.ONO, H.Matsui: "Jinko shijo Project U-Mart no Kyoiku katsudo", *system/seigyo/information*, 49, 7, 19-24, 2005.
- Kazuhisa Taniguchi: "Human ni yoru Kaso sakimono sijo jikkenn - U-Mart jikkenn report ", *-Ikoma keizai ronngi*, 3, 1, 17-31, 2005.
- Yoshinori Shiozawa: "Robott ikusei sangyo de kangaeru beki koto", *Toshimondai kenkyu*, 57, 9, 21-33, 2005.
- H.Kita, K.Taniguchi, I.Ono, H.Matsui: "Jinko shijo Project U-Mart no kyoiku katsudo", *system/seigyo/information*, 49, 7, 2005.
- H.Sato, Y.Koyama, K.Kurumatani, Y.Shiozawa, and H.Deguchi: "U-Mart: A Test Bed for Interdisciplinary Research in Agent Based Artificial Market", *Evolutionary Controversies in Economics*, 179-190, 2001.
- Yorikazu Takao, Isao Ono, Norihiko Ono: "Constructing Approximation Models Based on Agent-Based Simulations by Genetic Algorithms ", *Proceedings of Fourth International Conference on Computational Intelligence and Multimedia Applications*, 231-235, 2001.
- T.Terano, Y.Shiozawa, H.Deguchi, H.Kita, H.Matsui, H.Sato, and I.Ono: "U-Mart: An Artificial Market to Bridge the Studies on Economics and Multi-agent Systems", *Proceedings of Fourth Pacific Rim International Workshop on Multi-agents*, 371-385, 2001.

- H.Matsui, I.Ono, H .Sato, H.Deguchi, T, Terano, H.Kita, and Y.Shiozawa: "Learning Economics Principles from the Bottom by both Human and Software Agents- Outline of U-Mart Project", *-Proceedings of CASOS 2001 International Conference*, 97-99, 2001.
- H.Sato, H.Matsui, I.Ono, H.Kita, and T.Terano : "U-Mart Project: Learning Economic Principles from the Bottom by both Human and Software Agents", *Proceedings of the First International Workshop on Agent-based Approaches in Economic and Social Complex Systems* (AESCS-2001), 56-66, 2001.
- H.Sato, H.Matsui, I.Ono, H.Kita, T.Terano, H.Deguchi, and Y.Shiozawa: "U-Mart Project: Learning Economic Principles from the bottom by Both Human and Software Agents", *New Frontiers in Artificial Intelligence*, 121-131, 2002.
- H.Sato, H.Matsui, I.Ono, H.Kita, T.Terano, H.Deguchi, and Y.Shiozawa : "Case Report on U-Mart Experimental System: Competition of Software Agent and Gaming Simulation with Human Agents", *Agent-Based Approaches in Economics and Social Complex Systems, Joint JSAI 2001 Workshop Pst-Proceedings*, 167-178, 2002.
- T. Terano, Y.Shiozawa, H. Deguchi, Hajime Kita, H. Matsui, H. Sato, I. Ono and Y. Nakajima: "U-Mart: An Artificial Market Testbed for Economics and Multiagent Systems", *2nd International Workshop on Agent-based Approaches in Economics and Social Complex Systems*, 55-62, 2002.
- Hiroshi Deguchi, Takao Terano, Hajime Kita, Yoshinori Shiozawa, Robert Axtell, Katheleen Carley, Maksim Tsvetovat, Hiroshi Sato, Hiroyuki Matsui, Isao Ono, Yoshihiro Nakajima, Naoki Mori: "U-Mart International Experiment2003 (U MIE2003)", *NAACSOS2003 North American Association for Computational Social and Organizational Science Conference*, CD-ROM: NAACSOS_PAPERS _DAY3\ Sato_Hiroshi_s2_d3_p1.pdf, 2003.
- Hiroshi Deguchi, Takao Terano, Hajime Kita, Yoshinori Shiozawa, Robert Axtell, Katheleen Carley, Maksim Tsvetovat, Hiroshi Sato, Hiroyuki Matsui, Isao Ono, Yoshihiro Nakajima, Naoki Mori: "Report of UMIE2002 -Strategy and Rank Order of Submitted Machine Agents", *NAACSOS2003 (UMIE2003) North American Association for Computational Social and Organizational Science Conference*, CD-ROM: NAACSOS_PAPERS_DAY3\Sato_Hiroshi_s2_d3_p2.pdf, 2003.
- Hajime KITA, Hiroshi SATO, Naoki MORI, Isao ONO: "U-Mart System, Software for Open Experimnets of Artificial Market", *CIRA2003 IEEE Computational Intelligence in Robotics and Automation*, CD-ROM\papers\CIRA-SS07-3.pdf, 2003.
- Tomomi UEDA, Kazuhisa TANIGUCHI, Yoshihiro NAKAJIMA: "An Analysis of U-Mart Experiments by Machine and Human Agents", *CIRA2003 IEEE Computational Intelligence in Robotics and Automation*, CD-ROM\papers\CIRASS 07- 5.pdf, 2003.
- Yoshihiro NAKAJIMA, Tomomi UEDA: "Analysis of Submitted Agent to UMIE 2002- Influence of Spot Data and Oppornents on Agents", *NAACSOS2003 (UMIE2003) North American Association for Computational Social and Orga-*

*nizational Science Conference*, CD-ROM: NAACSOS_PAPERS_DAY3\ Nakajima, Ueda_Yoshihor, Tomomi_s2_d3.pdf, 2003.

- Hiroyuki Matsui, Kazuhisa Taniguchi, Yasuhiro Nakajima, Isao Ono, Hiroshi Sato, Naoki Mori, Hajime Kita, Takao Terano, Hiroshi Deguchi, Yoshinori Shiozawa: "U-Mart Project: New Research and Education Program for Market Mechanism", *ISAGA2003 International Simulation And Gaming Association (ISAGA) The 34th Annual Conference Hosted by Science Council of Japan (SCJ) and Japan Simulation And Gaming Association (JASAG)* , 2003.
- Kazuhisa Taniguchi, Yoshihiro Nakajima, Fumihiko Hashimoto: "A Report of U-Mart Experiments by Human Agents", *ISAGA2003 International Simulation And Gaming Association (ISAGA) The 34th Annual Conference Hosted by Science Council of Japan (SCJ) and Japan Simulation And Gaming Association (JASAG)*, 2003.
- Yoshihiro Nakajima, Isao Ono, Naoki Mori, Hiroyuki Matsui, Hiroshi Sato: "Elementary Property of U-Mart found by Submitted Agents to "U-Mart International Experiment" ", *ISAGA2003 International Simulation And Gaming Association (ISAGA) The 34th Annual Conference Hosted by Science Council of Japan (SCJ) and Japan Simulation And Gaming Association (JASAG)*, 2003.
- Isao Ono, Naoki Mori, Hiroshi Sato, Hajime Kita, Hiroyuki Matsui, Yoshihiro Nakajima: "U-Mart System Version 2: A Multi-Purpose Artificial Market Simulator", *AESCS'04*, CD-ROM, 2004.
- Hiroyuki Matsui, Yoshihiro Nakajima, Hiroshi Sato: "Performance of Machine Agents Submitted to U-Mart International Experiment 2004 (UMIE2004)", *AESCS04*, CD-ROM, 2004.
- Hiroshi Deguchi, Takao Terano, Hajime Kita, Yoshinori Shiozawa, Robert Axtell, Katheleen Carley, Maksim Tsvetovat, Hiroshi Sato, Hiroyuki Matsui, Isao Ono, Naoki Mori, Yoshihiro Nakajima: "Report of U-Mart International Experiment (UMIE2003 and UMIE 2004) – Strategy and Rank Order of Submitted Machine Agents", *NAACSOS*, CD-ROM, 2004.
- Hiroshi Sato, Isao Ono: "A Survey of the Research using U-Mart Experimental Environment", *AESCS04*, CD-ROM, 2004.
- Jungo Ueki, Yoshihiro Nakajima: "Analysis of Time Series Behaviors in High-Frequency Area Using Artificial Market", *NAACSOS*, CD-ROM, 2004.
- Yoshihiro Nakajima, Yoshinori Shiozawa: "Usefulness and feasibility of market maker in a thin market", *ICEES (International Conference Experiments in Economic Sciences)*, 2004.
- Yoshihiro Nakajima, Isao Ono, Hiroshi Sato, Naoki Mori, Hajime Kita, Hiroyuki Matsui, Kazuhisa Taniguchi, Hiroshi Deguchi, Takao Terano, Yoshinori Shiozawa: "Introducing Vertual Futures market System "U-Mart" ", *ICEES (International Conference Experiments in Economic Sciences)*, 2004.
- Jungo Ueki , Yoshihiro Nakajima: "Analyse the complexity of the financial time series using artificial market", *ICEES (International Conference Experiments in Economic Sciences)*, 2004.
- Kita, Ono, Mori, Sato, Matsui, Nakajima: "U-Mart Kaso keizai system no Genjo to Kongo", *JAWS (Third Joint Agent Workshops & Symposium)* 2004, 2004.

- Kita, Ono, Mori, Sato, Taniguchi, Matsui, Nakajima, Koyama, Ishiyama: "U-Mart Jinko sakimono shijo project ni okeru kyoiku katsudo", *SICE System joho bumon kouenkai SSI2004 (SICE Sympossium on Systems and Information)*, 2004.
- Koyama, Y., Ishiyama, K., Matsui, H. and Ono, I.: "Using U-Mart System for the Lecture of Economics", *4th Int'l Workshop on Agent-based Approaches in Economics and Social Complex Systems*, 2005.
- Yoshinori Shiozawa: "Making a Thin Market Intentionally: a Challenge of the U-MART Project", WEHIA, 2004.

Verbal Presentations

- Hiroshi Sato: "U-Mart niokeru choukikakakuhendou no toukeitekiseishitsu", Keis okujidoseigyo gakkai, 14thJiritsubunsan system symposium, pp.183-188, 2002.
- H.Kita, H.Deguchi, T.Terano: "Open gata jinkosijoU-Mart: Kouso, Seika, Tenbo", Denshijohotsusingakkai Gijutsukenkyuhoukoku [Jinkosijo to chishikisyo ri] (Shingakugihou Vol101, No535), pp.17-24, 2002.
- Y.Nakajima: "Jinkosijo to genjitu no sijo", Denshijohotsushingakkai Kenkyu houkoku [Jinkoshijo to chishikisyori] (Shingakugiho Vol101, No535), pp.71-78, 2002.
- Y.Nakajima, Y.Koyama: "Attempt to design institutions of market by using U-Mart System -A practice of interdisciplinary research- ", SICE 25th system kougakubukai kenkyukai (catalog NO.02PG0006), pp.133-138, 2002.
- U-Mart Organizing Comittee, U-Mart System Operation Committee: "U-Mart International Experiment 2002", SICE 25th system kougakubukai kenkyukai (catalog NO.02PG0006), pp.139-146, 2002.
- Takao Terano: "U-MartProject: Jinkoshijo kenkyu kara seidosekkei he", Shinkakeizaigakuronsyu 6th, pp.285-288, 2002.
- Yoshihiro Nakajima: "U-Mart wo mochiita korekara no kenkyukeikaku", Shinkak eizaigakkaironsyu 6th, pp.289-295, 2002.
- K.Taniguchi, H.Matsui, H.Deguchi, T.Igarashi: "Kyoiku tool toshiteno U-Mart: Keizaigaku Kyoiku deno katsuyo jirei", Shinkakeizaigakuronsyu No.6, pp.296-303, 2002.
- Hajime Kita, Hideo Yuasa: "Kyoiku tool to shiteno U-Mart: Kogaku kyoikudeno katsuyo jirei", Shinkakeizaigakuronsyu 6th, pp.304-308, 2002.
- Hiroshi Sato, Yusuke Koyama: "U-Mart2001 jikken hokoku oyobi kizon agent no bunrui", Shinkakeizaigakuronsyu 6th, pp.309-314, 2002.
- H.Takao, I.Ono, T.Ono: "Agent base simulation ni motoduku kinji model no shinkateki kouchiku", Shinkakeizaigakuronsyu 6th, pp.315-322, 2002.
- J.Ueki, N.Mori, H.Kai, N.Hukase, H.Sato, G.Goto, T.Ueda, A.Kumei, Y. Nakajima: "U-Mart niyoru simulation kenkyu", Shinkakeizaigakuronsyu 6th, pp.323-329, 2002.
- Hideo Yuasa, Hajime Kita, Tomohiko Kobayashi: "Project ensyu niyoru kyoiku jitsurei U-Mart niyoru kyoiku tool", Nihon kikaigakkai 2002, 2002.

- Hajime Kita: "U-Mart Project no syokai", FIT (joho gijutsu forum) 2002, OE1-2, pp. 65-66, 2002.
- Hajime Kita: "U-Mart no jouhoukeikyuiku heno riyo", SICE 26th system kougakubukai kenkyukai (catalog No.02PG0011) pp.7-12, 2002.
- Fumihiko Hashimoto, Tomomi Ueda, Yuko Kitazawa: "Ningenno jouhousyori-nouryoku ni motoduku kouritsuteki na jouhou teiji system", SICE 26th system kogakubukai kenkyukai (catalog No.02PG0011) pp.39-42, 2002.pp. 435-439, 2003.
- Naoki Mori, Isao Ono, Hiroyuki Matsui, Hiroshi Sato, Hajime Kita, Hiroshi Deguchi: "U-Mart System to Object sikou sekkei — Programing- U-Mart summer school report", SICE 26th system kougakubukai kenkyukai (catalog No. 02PG0011) pp.1-6, 2002.
- Isao Ono, Hiroshi Sato, Naoki Mori, Hajime Kita, Hiroyuki Matsui: "Syakai keizai simulation notameno software kaihatsu houhouron", Shinkakeizai gakkai 7th Tokyo (Sensyu Uni.) pp. 283-288, 2003.
- Hajime Kita: "Agent based model niyoru syakai sisutemu no rikai", Shinkakeizai gakkai 7th Tokyo (Sensyu Uni.) pp. 435-439, 2003.
- Yoshinori Shiozawa"U-Mart kara umareru atarasii keizaigaku", Shinkakeizai gakkai 7th Tokyo (Sensyu Uni.), 2003.
- Kazuhisa Taniguchi: "Gaming niyoru kakakukeisei mekanizumuno rikai -course ware toshitenoU-Mart", Shinkakeizaigakkai 7th Tokyo (Sensyu Uni.) pp. 289-292, 2003.
- Y.Nakajima, H.Kita, I.Ono, N.Mori, H.Sato, H.Matsui, T.Terano, H.Deguchi, Y.Koyama: "Jinko sakimono sijou U-Mart no syoukai", SICE souhatsu natuno gakkou poster happyou, 2004.
- Isao Ono , Naoki Mori, Hiroshi Sato, Hajime Kita, Hiroyuki Matsui, Yoshihiro Nakajima: "U-Mart System new sever no syoukai", Shinkakeizaigakkai at Fukui p.312, 2004.
- Y.Nakajima , I.Ono, N.Mori, H.Deguchi, H.Ishiyama, H.Matsui: "U-Mart Version2.0 wo riyoushita human agent niyoru kabushikisakimonotori hiki jikkenn — gaming no syuhou wo riyousita taikenngatagakusyuu to seidokennkyuu — " Shinkakeizaigakkai at Fukui pp.285-292, 2004.
- Kazuhisa Taniguchi: "Vit no renzokukasetu nikannsuru ichikousatsu", Shinka keizaigakuronsyu, 9th, pp.89-96, 2005.
- Yoshinori Shiozawa: "Stress test niha 5siguma jitaiwo kanngaeyou", Syunkan keirijouhou (1075), p1, 2005.

Books and Publications

- K. Taniguchi, Y. Nakajima, F. Hashimoto: "A Report of U-Mart Experiments by Human Agents", R. Shiratori, K. Arai, F. Kato, *Gaming, Simulations, and Society: Research Scope and Perspective*, Springer, pp.49-57, 2004.
- Yoshinori Shiozawa: "Fukuzatsukeikeizaigaku no genzai", Shiozawa Yoshinori, Shiozawa Yoshinori, 2004, PP.53-125, 2004.

- Kazuhisa Taniguchi, Yoshihiro Nakajima, Fumihiko Hashimoto: “A Report of U-Mart Experiments by Human Agents”, R. Shiratori, K. Arai, F. Kato, *Gaming, Simulations and Society: Research Scope and Perspective*, Springer-Verlag Tokyo, pp.49-57, 2005.
- Kazuhisa Taniguchi, Yoshihiro Nakajima, Fumihiko Hashimoto: “A Report of U-Mart Experiments as an Educational Courseware”, Terano, T., Kita, H., Arai, K. Deguchi, H. , *Agent-Based Simulation - from Modeling Methodologies to Real World Applications* , -Springer-Verlag Tokyo, pp.82-88, 2005.
- Hajime KITA, Yoshihiro NAKAJIMA, Isao ONO: An Artificial Market Approach to Institutional Design for Thin Markets, *SICE-ICASE International Joint Conference 2006*, pp. 4596-4600 (2006).

# Bibliography


[1] Ikutarou Aihou, *Technical Analysis of Stock Market (In Japanese only, Japanese Title: Kabushikisouba no tekunikaru Bunseki,* Nihonkeizai Shinbunsya, 1989.

[2] Takeshi Goto and Yoshinori Shiozawa, *Classification of Trader's Conduct (In Japanese only, Japanese Title: Toreda no Koudou no Bunrui),* U-Mart Kansai Kenkyukai, 10, Dec, 1999.

[3] Hitotsubashi University, Syougaku Kenkyuuka edit., *Future Market of New Century (In Japanese only, Japanese Title: Shinseki no SakimonoSijou),* touyoukeizai Shinpousya

[4] Kiyoshi Izumi and Kazuhiro Ueda, *Introduction of Artificial Market, (In Japanese only, Japanese Title: Jinkousijou Nyumon,)* Jouhousyorigakkai Jinkoutinou Kennkyuukai Houkoku, Vol.99, pp9-17,2000.

[5] Kiyoshi Izumi, *Artificial Market (In Japanese Only, Japanese Title: Jinkousijou),* Morikita Syuppann 2003.

[6] D. Kahneman and A. Tversky. "Prospect theory: An analysis of decision under risk", *Econometrica*, Vol. 47, , 1979.

[7] Hisao Kanamori, Kenjirou Ara and Tikashi Moriguchi, edits., *Dictionary of Economy (In Japanese Only, Japanese Title: Keizaijiten)* . Yuuhikaku, 1998.

[8] Hajime Kita, *Introduction of U-Mart (In Japanese only, Japanese Title: U-mart Nyumon).* Included in Documents of U-Mart2000 Agente Kaitatu Kit, 2000.

[9] Hajime Kita, Hiroshi Sato, Naoki Mori, and Isao Ono. "U-Mart System, Software for Open Experiments of Artificial Market". In *CIRA2003 IEEE Computational Intelligence in Robotics and Automation*, pp. CIRA–SS07–3.pdf. 2003.

[10] Yusuke Koyama, *Educational Text of U-Mart, (In Japanese only, Japanese Title: U-Mart Kyouikuyo Tekisuto,).* U-Mart Kousyukai, Distributed in Osaka City University, 2001.

[11] Blake LeBaron, W. Brian Arthur, and Richard Palmer. "Time series properties of an artificial stock market", *Journal of Economics Dynamics and Control*, pp. 1487–1516, 1999.

[12] Hiroyuki Matui, Kazuhisa Taniguchi, Yasuhiro Nakajima, Isao Ono, Hiroshi Sato, Naoki Mori, Hajime Kita, Takao Terano, Hiroshi Deguchi, and Yoshinori Shiozawa, "Umart Project: New Research and Education Program for Market Mechanism", 2003. ISAGA2003, International Simulation And Gaming Association (ISAGA), The 34th Annual Conference Hosted by Science Council of Japan (SCJ) and Japan Simulation And Gaming Association (JASAG).

[13] Michio Morishima, *Economics of No Resources Country, (In Japanese Only, Japanese Title: Mushigenkoku no Keizaigaku),* Iwanami Shoten, 1984.

[14] Maureen O'Hara, *Market Microstructure Theory,* Blackwell Publishers, 1995.

[15] Keiichi Omura, Jun Uno, Hidetaka Kawakita and Masashi Toshino, *Micro Structure of Stock Market, (In Japanese only, Japanese Title: Kabushiki Sijou no MaikuroSutorakuture),* Nihon Keizai Sinbunsya, 1998.

[16] A. Shleifer. *Inefficient Markets—An Intoroduction to Behavioral Finance.* Oxford University Press, 2000.

[17] Saichirou Sumionoe, edit., *Nihon Keisenshi (In Japanese only, Japanese Title: A history of Jananese Keisen),* Nihon Keizai Sinbunsya, 1978.

[18] Kan Takamori, *Basic Theory of Modern Finance (In Japanese only, Japanese Title: Gendai Fainansu no Kiso Riron)*, Toyou Keizai Sinpousya, 2002.

[19] Hideki Takayasu and Misako Takayasu, Econophysics, (In Japanese only, Japanese Title: Ekonofizikusu), Nihon Keizai Shinbunsya,2001.

[20] H. Takayasu, T. Hirabayashi, H. Miura, and K. Hamada. "Statical properties of deterministic threshold elements". *Physica A*, pp. 127–134, 1992.

[21] Kazuhisa Taniguchi, *Seminar Documents, (In Japanese only, Japanese Title: Ensyu Shiryou)*, Distributed in the Conference of Japan Association for Evolutionary Economics, 2001.

[22] Kazuhisa Taniguchi, *U-Mart as an Educational Kit, (In Japanese Only, Japanese Title: Kyouiku Kit toshitemo U-Mart).* Distributed in the Conference of Japan Association for Evolutionary Economics, 2001.

[23] Kazuhisa Taniguchi, Yoshihiro Nakajima, and Fumihiko Hashimoto. "A Report of U-Mart Experiments by Human Agents". In R.Shiratori, K.Arai, and F.Kato, editors, *Gaming, Simulations, and Society -Research Scope and Perspective-*, pp. 49–57. Springer-Verlag Tokyo, 2005.

[24] Richard H. Thaler, *The Winner's Curse —Paradoxes and Anomalies of Economic Life*. Princeton University Press, New Jersey, 1992.

[25] Hiroshi Usami, *Introduction of Future Market (In Japanese Only, Japanese Title: Nyumon Sakimono Shijou)*, Touyou Keizai Sinpousya, 2000.

[26] Robert Axelrod, *The Complexity of Cooperation*, Princeton University Press, 1997

[27] Edward Chanceller, *Devil Take the Hindmost; A History of Financial Speculation*. Farrar, Straus and Giroux, 1999.

[28] J,D. Duffie, *Futures Markets*, Prentice Hall, 1989.

[29] Daniel Friedman & Shyam Sunder, *Experimental Methods: A Primer for Economics,* Cambrdige University Press, 1994.

[30] Nigel Gilbert and Klaus G. Troitzsch, *Simulation for the Social Scientist,* 1st Ed. 1999, 2nd Ed. 2005.
[31] Joachim Goldberg and Rudiger von Nitzsch, *Behavioral Finance.* German Ed. by FinazBuch Verlag, 1999, English Ed. By John Wiley 2001.
[32] Cathy Stein Greenblat, *Designin Gams and Simulations.* Sage Publications. 1988.
[33] Robert A. Haugen, *The Inefficient Stock Market: What Pays Off and Why,* 2nd Ed., 2002.
[34] Benoit B. Mandelbrot, *Fractals and Scaling in Finance*, NewYork, Springer Verlag, 1997.
[35] Benoit B. Mandelbrot and Richard L. Hudson, *The (Mis)Behavior of Markets, A Fractal View of Risk, Ruin, and Reward.* New York, Basic Books, 2004.
[36] Rosario N. Mantegna and H. Eugene Stanley, *An Introduction to Econophysics: Correlations and Complexity in Finance.* Cambridge University Press, 1999.
[37] Ross M.Miller, *Experimental Economics/How We Can Build Better Financial Markts,* John Wiley, 2002.
[38] Edgar E. Peters, *Chaos and Order in the Capital Markets: A New View of Cycles , Prices and Market Volatilit,* New York, John Wiley, 1991.
[39] Osaka Securities Exchange, All of the Future Trading, (In Japanese only, Japanese Title: Sakimono Torihiki no Subete), Osaka Securities Exchange, 2000.

# Index

MIX
Papier aus verantwortungsvollen Quellen
Paper from responsible sources
FSC® C105338

If you have any concerns about our products,
you can contact us on
**ProductSafety@springernature.com**

In case Publisher is established outside the EU,
the EU authorized representative is:
**Springer Nature Customer Service Center GmbH**
**Europaplatz 3, 69115 Heidelberg, Germany**

Printed by Libri Plureos GmbH
in Hamburg, Germany